One Reason

There is only

One Reason

why people will like you

An overview of likeability

Marcel Elfers

Cover artwork: Marcel Elfers

ISBN-13: 978-1530903450
ISBN-10: 1530903459

2nd edition © 2016
The second edition expanded the chapter information processes and main themes. Blind spots have been added. Some improvements have been made in word selection and sentence construction.

Printed by CreateSpace, an Amazon.com Company

Nosce Te Ipsum

For you,

willing to listen,

to be the best you can be.

Acknowledgments

I wish to thank my late father

who taught me to look and listen.

Who should read this book

One Reason has been written with teenagers and young adults in mind.

This is for you
and your chance to know what I did not at your age.

Anyone benefits from the insight offered. The rules of engagement are universal, for all ages, and show how to be your own best friend.

Author's Note

According to the Enneagram, we behave in one of nine behavioral patterns. These patterns are built on a core perspective established in our childhood. They are *distinct* and *consistent* and therefore identifiable.

Look and Listen!

We can distinguish one pattern from the other by observing behavior styles and listen to what people say. This provides us insight in a person's core perspective, needs, strengths, and weaknesses.

Three rules:
1. we always talk about what is important to us
2. we give others what we need the most
3. we hurt others with what hurts us the most

It is my hope you will recognize and relate to these patterns in yourself as well as others. When you do, your journey started.

The content has been kept to the basics. My intent is to provide a foundation for understanding others, pique interest to learn more, and to realize why others see things differently.

For more accurate and detailed insights regarding this fascinating subject, I suggest you read my first book "We are the same; it's the details that differ."

Note to parents and teachers

When we were children, we developed a perspective, a core need, and learned to act to meet that need.

As children and young adults, we were not able to express how we viewed our parents and the world. We did not understand what we needed the most. We were too young, did not have the insight, nor the ability to verbalize such needs.

Children behave and express themselves in distinct patterns based on their perspective. Behaviors and expressions reveal perspective, how they view you, and their place in the family. This point of view is projected onto other role models and later, in our adulthood, onto the world as a whole.

Everyone benefits from these insights. However, parents and teachers are in the unique position to direct and redirect our next generation.

On a personal note, I am a Type Five.

A Five's perspective is "the world is unreliable." They compensate by observing from a distance and learning to understand the world. They become inquisitive, information junkies, and often develop specialized know how. Once a Five has figured out what they needed to know the most, they feel compelled to share what they know.

This book is a result of that process.
Enjoy.

About the Author

Marcel Elfers was born and raised in Haarlem, the Netherlands. He moved to the United States in the mid-eighties as a Physical Therapist. He has always been observant and the need to figure people out. Why does he do this? Why does she say that?

He became a Master Profiler through written communication and authored his first book "We are the same; it's the details that differ" in 2015. This book was inspired by Elliot Rodger's manifesto. He was a young man whose inner conflict drove him to do the unthinkable. His detailed manifesto laid out his life and he described a known, distinct, and consistent pattern with stunning clarity.

Elliot Rodger's inner conflict was "I am the best" and "I am excluded". He described his life in detail in his manifesto. The conflict between feeling important and being excluded was the main driver behind his violent act. May he and his victims rest in peace. May all families involved find the strength to cope.

Marcel Elfers is available for speaking engagements, family dynamics and behavioral profile consultations, threat assessments, and Precision Personnel Placement. He provides training through online and onsite courses.

Contents

If you go out looking for a friend,
you discover they are scarce.

If you go out to be a friend,
you find them everywhere.

- Zig Ziglar

Introduction

"One Reason" is about life.

One Reason explains we need others to succeed and means we need to make friends. We gain alliances and cooperation by making others feel good about themselves. Therefore, we must meet their core needs. It turns out our core need established itself in our childhood and permeates through our lives.

We are born with natural abilities and are influenced by our environment. *Nature* and *Nurture.* As a child, we learn to view our role models in a certain way. Based on our interaction with our parent(s), family, and friends, we learn to see ourselves in a specific way. This gives us an internal dialogue and a core perspective, which provides us with a core need to be met.

There are nine core perspectives[1] resulting in nine distinct and consistent behavioral patterns. Through observation and listening what others say, or *Look* and *Listen*, you will be able to identify a distinct pattern.

Awareness of patterns is vital for yourself as well as others. You can only make changes when you see your personal undesirable habits unfold. You can recognize patterns in others and understand *what*, *why*, and *how* they think, identify their core perspective, core need, strengths, and weaknesses. And allows us to influence with integrity.

To understand others is a gift and allows us to meet their core needs. You will make friends, create alliances, and gain cooperation.

I wish you to have this gift. Your happiness and success depend on it.

---

[1] Riso, Don Richard, and Hudson, Russ: *Personality Types: Using the Enneagram for Self-Discovery* (1996)

Success

**Your success depends on
how well you work with others.**
- Jennifer Hudson

They work with you when they like you.

**People forget what you said, what you did,
but never forget how they made you feel.**
- Maya Angelou

They like you when you make them feel good.

Four seconds

An important universal rule is

The first four seconds
sets the tone for the next four hours.

Imagine you are at home sitting on the floor playing with your two year old. The front door opens and your husband comes home from work. He whistles a tune, walks over to you, picks you up, kisses you and touches your cheek. He cannot wait to pick up his daughter too, kisses, and hugs her.

In contrast, the front door opens, he slams it shut, dumps his tool bag in the hallway, curses, and walks passed you to grab himself a beer to watch some sports. He just set an unhappy tone for the next four hours.

The first four seconds set the general mood for the next few hours. This rule applies at home, school, work, and anywhere else.

Dogs are notorious for tail wagging and excited greetings when you get home. And that makes us feel good.

One Reason

There is only one reason why you like someone:

**You like someone because
they make you feel good about yourself.**

To be appreciated for who you are is the most powerful thing we can hear. Turn this around,

**Others will like you because
you make them feel good about themselves.**

The question is:
"What makes you feel good about yourself?"
What do you want to hear the most?

The other question is:
"What makes others feel good about themselves?"
What do they want to hear the most?

Interestingly, most people cannot answer this question.

Three times three

We have to find answers to the question "What makes us feel good?" And that is exactly what we are going to explore. Verbal and non-verbal expressions reflect on our core need. We need to learn to pay attention to how others behave and listen to what they say.

Observation will provide us with the gist of a personality and more exposure will fill in the details. To change the subject:

Picture an automobile.

You selected a car of your liking. And others theirs. We know every car has four wheels, steering wheel, engine, brakes, and a cabin. Some pictured a sedan, a SUV, a quad cab, a formula I, a convertible, small, big, color etc.

The point is, we can observe the gist of a car immediately and fill in the details by looking "under the hood." And that is exactly what we are going to do with personality types. We find the gist, and fill in details as we continue to look and listen.

There are three main *behavioral style* groups containing three *core perspectives*. The behavioral style groups are 378[2], 612, and 945. Each perspective, also referred to as a "type 3, type 7, and type 8", emphasizes their own point of view.

The nine (9) core perspectives reference to nine (9) core needs[3]. Perspectives and consequent behavioral patterns are distinct and will be discussed in upcoming chapters.

---

[2] Read as "Three, Seven, and Eight"
[3] according to the Enneagram

Group 378

Group 378 focus is "to get what we want." They tend to be self-confident, self-assured, forceful, emphatic, aggressive, and forth coming. As a group, they are self-oriented and pursue personal needs.

Group 378 believes
- I am important
- I set my rules
- What I say matters
- You need to listen to me

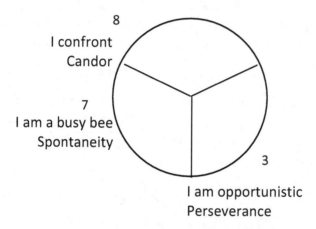

Figure 1: Assertives: theme and strength

The three types share their themes and emphasize their own. The extreme unhealthy assertives may be sociopathic and grossly overstep social boundaries.

Group 612

Group 612 is the compliant group. They focus on weighing morals and values of society as a whole. They are committed, loyal, steadfast, devoted, obedient, traditional, and conforming. As a group, they feel good adhering to existing principles and may enforce their standards onto others and effectively remove their choice.

Group 612 believes
- I am conforming
- I follow rules
- I want you to embrace my ideals
- I enforce standards

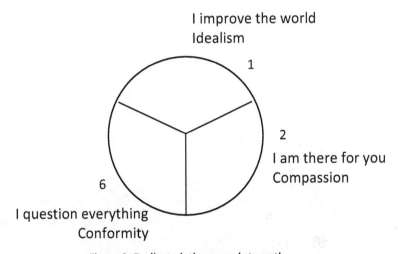

Figure 2: Dedicated: theme and strength

The three types share their themes and emphasize their own. In extreme unhealthy individuals, they may become fanatical and even blindly obedient.

Group 945

Group 945 is the withdrawn group. They need to find their place in the world and weigh ideals versus reality. They tend to be reserved, introverted, self-inhibiting, solitary, thoughtful, and standoffish. As a group, they stay in the background, are non-confrontational, and think before they speak.

Group 945 believes
- I am not important
- I need understanding
- I need to fit in
- If you want to, listen to me

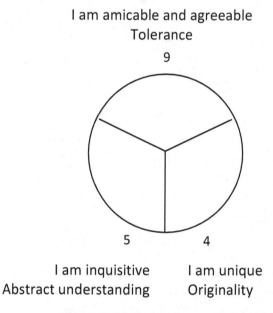

I am amicable and agreeable
Tolerance
9

5   4

I am inquisitive   I am unique
Abstract understanding   Originality

Figure 3: Withdrawns: theme and strength

The three types share their themes and emphasize their own. They may become nihilistic, isolate, and may even disengage from the world.

Feel good

Each type feels good when their perspective is *validated* and their behaviors *appreciated*.

**The quality of a relationship is measured
by how much the needs of those involved are met.**

- Dr. Phil

Each group share three needs. Each type needs to hear their specific need validated as it relates to their main theme:

Main: *We need to get what we want*	
3	That I am good, even excel, at what I am doing
7	That you support me getting what I want
8	That I am safe and protected

Main: *We weigh morals and values*	
6	That I am supported and have you help me decide
1	That I am prudent, rational, and support my opinion
2	That I am loved and appreciated for being good

Main: *We want to be acknowledged*	
9	That I am listened to and my opinion is heard
4	That I am included and accepted for who I am
5	That you listen to what I have figured out

Fives feel people are unreliable and compensate by observing from a distance. They feel safe when they understand the world and therefore they study. On a personal note, I finally believe I understand personality types and what, why, and how they think. A good friend said, "I was talking with my neighbor about how your book truly helped my husband and I understand each other." It does not get any better than being a positive influence on others. Hard work, knowledge, and insight validated. A core need was met.

27

Our core needs must be met. There are many other needs we want met, but our core need must be met for us to feel validated.

People whose core need is resisted, challenged, or denied will feel rejected for who they are.

It is important to realize what the core needs are in relationship dynamics. What does your partner need to hear? What should you avoid? Learn to emphasize strengths and de-emphasize weaknesses.

We all want to be *appreciated* for who we are, feel *safe* with the ones we are with, and make *independent* choices we deem best for us. These are our three universal needs.

- Acceptance: need for positive self-regard
    - Procreation: need for family and support
    - Romance: need for emotional acceptance
    - Socialization: need to enjoy life with others
    - Vengeance: need to confront provocations
- Independence: need for self-reliance
    - Status: need for respect
    - Power: need for to make independent choices
    - Integrity: need to be good
    - Idealism: need to be just
- Safety: need for security
    - Ownership: need to collect and exchange
    - Curiosity: need for understanding
    - Food: need to survive
    - Order: need to anticipate

Each Type requires all universal needs to be met, will pursue them, and will emphasize one over the other two within the universal needs group.

I am a 5w6 and emphasize finding the truth (to feel safe) and weighing ideals (what I want) versus reality (do I need it?).

Bonds

Every thought, every idea, every action we take shifts around our number one need: *to be validated*. Validation means acceptance, finding endorsement, and feeling approved off. Our ultimate pay off is to be appreciated for who we are. Our validation depends on

the quality of bonds
we create with other people.

Group 378 validate themselves. They are self-approving and feel good about themselves. Their focus is on self-promotion, self-fulfillment, and self-assertion. The bonds they create are superficial.
I get what I want. You follow me and stay out of my way.

Group 612 feel validated when they adhere to their convictions. They feel good following existing rules or create new ones. Their focus is on social responsibility, conformity, and relating to others. The bonds they create are morality based and doing things right.
I determine standards, adhere, and enforce them; appreciate me for doing things the right way.

Group 945 feel validated through approval of others. They feel good when others acknowledge and appreciate them. Their focus is on self-awareness, abstract understanding, and tolerance. The bonds they create with others are based on awareness and reality.
This is who I am; appreciate me for who I am.

Life is much easier when your learn to recognize the three core groups and understand their specific needs.

Life is simple.

However, "*How* do we figure out *what* someone needs to hear to feel validated?"

Here is how

Our core perspective gives us a core need. We develop a distinct behavioral pattern to fulfill this need. And behaviors can be observed.

The core perspective of a Two is "I feel unloved." They compensate by earning love and appreciation by being good to others. They are warm-hearted, people-oriented, flirtatious, and do things for you.

The Type Two example shows how perspective and behavior stack on top of each other like building blocks:
- Thinks: feels unloved
- Wants: to be loved
- Does: earn love by being good to others
- Needs: to hear they are loved and appreciated

A Two *needs* to hear you appreciate them for what they did for you. The Two, in the 612 group, also *wants* to hear you support them making decisions (6) and they did the right thing helping you (1).

A Two translates appreciation into "I am loved for being good." They feel validated and good about themselves. You just made a friend.

Our number one need is
to be appreciated for who we are.

To deny a core need is to deny the core of someone's being.

Our number one fear is
rejection for who we are.

Repetitive rejection for who we are, or validation denial, makes us feel unworthy and inevitably leads to resentment[4].

---

[4] Resentment is the number one indicator of a failing relationship

Look and Listen!

The foundation of our behavioral building blocks are

- core perspective →
- core need →
- behavioral pattern

We must have our core need met to make us feel worthy and confident. We always reveal ourselves because our behavioral patterns are consistent and distinct. We talk about our needs *(= expression)* and have to act *(= behave)* for our needs to be met.

The foundation for our behaviors is our core perspective. Turn this around and realize the recognition of a distinct behavioral pattern refers back to a core perspective. Perspective leads to behavior and therefore behavior points back to perspective.

- observe behavior→
- listen →
- core perspective

Observe behaviors, listen to what is said, identify a distinct pattern, recognize a core perspective and core need. In other words, you can understand where someone is coming from.

Note to parents: Children and young adults cannot verbalize how they view their parents, others, and the world. With this book, parents are handed a tool to identify a child's core perspective. Observe what they do and listen to what they say. A parent who identifies a child's core perspective understands their core need. Insight lays the foundation to meet their core need. Validation generates self-esteem and is a gift for you and your child.

Reveal ourselves

We reveal ourselves by what we do *(behave)*, don't *(avoid)*, and say *(express)*. We think and feel based on our point of view. And we cannot help but say and act on what we think.

Here is perspective of type Two again:
- unloved
- to be loved
- earn love by being good

A Two must be good to others. They attend to the needs of others *(do)* and repress their own needs *(don't)*. The needs of others is simply more important to a Two. You recognize them as they are overtly warm-hearted and make themselves needed.

> ## When people show you who they are, believe them.
>
> - Loretta Lynch, AG 2015

Volunteer nurse Kacie Hickox returned from Sierra Leone where she worked to fight the Ebola outbreak with Doctors without Borders. The U.S. had two Ebola deaths upon her return and Governor Christie forced her into quarantine. Kacie Hickox stated, and rightfully so, to quarantine had no merit.

A friend posted the following on Facebook:
"If I came home with the tiniest chance of giving someone else an awful disease... I'd self-quarantine for at least 21 days *(= being good to others). Keeping* others safe *would be* more important *to me (= others' needs more important) than my 'rights'."*

The Type Two perspective clearly shines through *(say)*: "I must be good and repress my own needs."

Type One grew up with criticism and compensate by striving to do better to avoid criticism. They learn to set their own standards and believe they know right from wrong. As adults, they may become critical and judgmental when others do not do what they see as "right." Consequently, each type has its own main theme:

Main themes[5]

3	I must succeed, act successful and repress feeling worthless
7	I am a busy bee and repress my anxiety
8	I am bossy and repress feeling vulnerable

6	I question everything and repress personal judgment
1	I judge right from wrong and act nice repressing resentment
2	I am good to others and repress my own needs

9	I am agreeable and repress personal preferences
4	I feel excluded and repress personal strengths
5	I need to understand and repress emotional attachment

There are many ways we expose ourselves. Trivial comments often reveal underlying details:

"How was New York?" I replied "NY is coming up in May; I am preparing the presentation right now." She texted back: "Fun! You'll be on the other side of the States. One end to the other!"

Why mention the obvious? She moved from Montana to South Carolina and the comment reflected on her own recent experience. Remember, trivial to you has significance to them.

People say exactly what they mean.
- Marcel Elfers 2005

Here is a simple request:
Before you turn the page, ...*think of five people*...

---

[5] A consistent habitual pattern

Question:
Isn't it true, your list of five people has a certain sequence of importance? The most important is first and the least important, but still important, last.

We have a very strong tendency to think and talk about what is most important to us first.

Imagine you are outside with some friends and a red convertible drives too fast. Friend A says, "That's dangerous." B says "Hot car." C says, "Must be cold." All approach the same subject from a different angle. The angle for A is safety, for B it is image, and for C the driver's experience. Each comment revealed what was important to them.

We always talk about that what is important to us.

Most people find it difficult to talk about themselves and much easier to say things about others. We judge others and think we define them. Reality is, *we define ourselves.*

Ask friend A what she likes about friend B. She answered with "He is kind, reliable, and trustworthy." Her answer resonates with what she likes herself and agrees with. She just revealed a little about herself.

What if she said, "He is arrogant and condescending." She just told us she does not appreciate such qualities.

We always reveal ourselves, no matter the circumstance. When you are on the dating scene, your date will put their best foot forward for the first six to eight weeks after which they will fall back on behaviors they know best. Your date treats you well as (s)he has a vested interest in you. They reveal who they are by how they treat others like the hostess, waiters, bartenders, a stranger saying hi, the valet etc. Just realize, that's what is in store for you in "eight" weeks.

1. What is the "One Reason" concept[6]?
2. Why "Look and Listen?"
3. What do we talk about the most?

_____

_____

_____

_____

_____

_____

_____

_____

_____

_____

_____

_____

_____

_____

_____

_____

_____

_____

_____

_____

_____

_____

_____

_____

_____

[6] answers page 120

Perspective test

Behavioral style and what you say point to your perspective.

Score 3 for what you relate to the most (A, B, or C). If you relate to two of them, score a 3 and a 2. Do the same for XYZ.
This test is very limited but may give you some direction[7].

Behavioral Style

A	I tend to be independent, assertive, and get what I want myself. I make things happen, favor action, and don't let others get in my way. I work hard.	
B	I tend to be a loner, quiet, and like to be by myself. I prefer to stay out of the lime light. I solve most problems by thinking things through first.	
C	I tend to be responsible, reliable, and pay attention to what is good and fair. I will sacrifice and do what is right or expected.	

Social Style

X	I am an engaging optimist with a glass is half-full attitude. Things will work out, so why worry? I love people and like to make them happy.	
Y	I have strong feelings and tend to share them readily. I may be guarded when not sure where I stand. I want others to feel they way I feel.	
Z	I like to control myself. I don't share my feelings much and like to work alone. I tend to keep my distance when upset.	

Two 3's combine to AX, AY, AZ, BX, etc.. They refer to one of nine core perspectives and a distinct behavioral pattern[8].

---

[7] See addendum "Test results"
[8] See page 45 figure 5

Three words

We reveal our perspective through thought expression. Our word selection has emotional value and we relate to certain words more so than others. This is why we use them in the first place.

- Thoughts become
- Words

Read all words in the table below and mark the group you relate to the most with a 3. The second most important group with a 2.

Prudent Objective Realistic	Different Unique Gentle	Strong Empowering Forth-coming
Responsible Trustworthy Dependable	Loving Caring Giving	Intelligent Insightful Competent
Independent Humble Forgiving	Spontaneous Confident Busy bee	Admirable Desirable Charming

Words are expressed thoughts and thought is perspective[9].

Remember, Type Two's perspective is "I feel unloved" and earn love and appreciation by being good to others. They are generous with hugs and use flattery. Therefore, a person who relates to "loving, caring, giving" may have revealed their core perspective[10] as an "Altruist."

- Words →
- Perspective

---

[9] See addendum "Word selection"
[10] It is not this simple but the principle is valid.

Thought is destiny

We have an internal dialogue *(thought)* and is what we tell ourselves. From this belief system, we develop a perspective, how we see ourselves, the world, and how we fit in. We will learn to express what we think *(words)* and act out what we say *(behavior)*. We will repeat what we know best *(habit)* and suddenly, we became *who* and *what* we thought we are *(destiny)*.

In other words:
- Thoughts become
- Words become
- Behavior becomes
- Habit becomes
- Destiny

We become who we think we are

A Type Eight grew up in an unsafe environment where weakness was used against them. This made them feel vulnerable and compensate by presenting themselves as strong and domineering.

- Thought: Who is going to violate me?
- Words: I protect myself and the underdog
- Behavior: I present myself as strong
- Habit: takes charge
- Destiny: authoritarian

We make choices we believe are best given our circumstances. How we see ourselves and what we believe our destiny should be, is exactly what we get. We "yes our way to where we are."

We get what we believe we deserve

One mindless word or action becomes a child's inner voice, is silently repeated over and over again, and acted upon. Then we repeat what we know best and behavior becomes habitual.

Personality is
a repetitive response to our internal dialogue.

The only question is:
which mindless word or action will have the most significant impact?

A child was adopted at birth. At age four, her adoptive mother committed suicide. Her adoptive father did not forgive himself and withdrew. She felt unloved and ignored. She learned she received praise and recognition when she did something good first. Her core perspective became: I must be good first before they love me. This is freely translated into "to earn love by being good to others."

Your parental word, action, and inaction becomes your child's destiny. Think about that for one moment:

Your word, their destiny.

It is best to be a positive influence and live by the nine core strengths:

- Be persistent
- Be enthusiastic
- Be forthright
- Be loyal
- Be fair
- Be compassionate
- Be who you are
- Be tolerant
- Be competent

Our childhood compensatory strategies will be used in a more sophisticated manner in our adulthood.

Childhood	Adulthood
• my parents were unreliable	• the world is unreliable
• I observe to understand	• I observe to understand

In essence, the world becomes a role model substitute. Next time someone treats you unfairly, just realize they are saying to you what they said or needed to say to their parent(s).

Behavior starts for one reason and continues for another.

We give others what we need the most. The Five's perspective is to understand the world. A Five is inquisitive and needs abstract understanding. Their angle is "applied knowledge is power."
A Five being good means to a Five "to share what you have learned." They are teachers and tend to explain things in a systematic manner.

- I must understand
- I will give you understanding

I am a Five and an avid pool player. I love to figure the game out and then explain pool principles to other players. Need to understand the "diamond system?" Ask me, and I will tell you.

Pay attention to what someone gives others. They are revealing their personal core need and core perspective.

Interesting tidbit: It takes time and energy to observe the world and discover patterns in order to feel safe. Five's energy is drained when they are in new circumstances. Therefore, Fives prefer predictability and go to the same restaurant ordering the same meal instead of trying something new. They laugh when I tell a Five that.

Three Rules

We tend to live by three rules and they shine through in our behavioral choices.

1. we always talk about what is important to us
2. we give others what we need the most
3. we hurt others with what hurts us the most

1. We talk about what is important to us
People will always talk about what is important to them and reveal themselves because of this very principle. All we need to do is Look and Listen[11].

2. We give others what we need the most
We have one core need to be met and believe others need that too.

A Type Nine doesn't feel important enough to be listened to. They fear being abandoned and alone in the world. They learn to be amicable, agreeable, and want tranquility. Their conflict avoidance gives others what they need the most: peace and quiet.

3. We hurt others with what hurts us the most
We believe what hurts us will hurt others as well and we use what hurts us to hurt others.

A type Three must be seen as a success and seeks performance acknowledgment. They thrive on hearing they did well and excel at whatever they do. A Three will be hurt when called a loser instead of a winner. Threes hurt others by calling them losers.

---

[11] See page 34 car example

Summary

The thread is to understand[12] others, understand their needs, and influence with integrity.

- success depends on how well you work with others
- make others feel good and gain a friend
- they feel good when their core need is met
- to figure out their core need
    - observe behavioral patterns
    - listen to what they say
- link behaviors and expression to perspective
- perspective reveals core need

---

[12] my Five perspective is shining through with the word "understand."

4. Define "Personality"

5. Why does thought become destiny?

6. Describe the pattern from birth to childhood

_____

_____

_____

_____

_____

_____

_____

_____

_____

_____

_____

_____

_____

_____

_____

_____

_____

_____

_____

_____

_____

_____

_____

_____

_____

_____

_____

_____

_____

Enneagram

Behavioral Pathway

We develop a perspective and behavioral style based on a developmental route. This is our behavioral pathway, if you will.

We are born with natural abilities and influenced by our environment. We identify with our role models and set our perspective accordingly. We develop a processing style and ego-defense mechanisms. Our behavioral and social style eventually leads to a distinct behavioral pattern. We can understand "what, why, and how" we think based on pattern recognition.

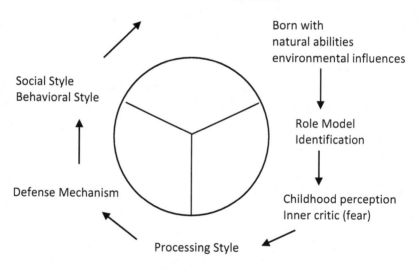

Distinct Behavioral Pattern

1-3	Healthy
4-6	Average
7-9	Unhealthy

Figure 4: Behavioral Pathway

Model

The Enneagram is a dynamic and systematic model mapping behavioral clusters. It links behaviors to universal and core needs.

The model maps
- what we want
- how we get what we want
- how we present ourselves

The model is built in Triads with nine numbered core perspectives. The numbers are no reflection of higher, lower, good, bad, better, or worse. They are meant to be abstract, meaningless, and could have been named A through I.

There is only perspective.

The model helps us identify core needs, strengths, and weaknesses through behavioral clusters. We need to study, understand, and commit parts of the model to memory.

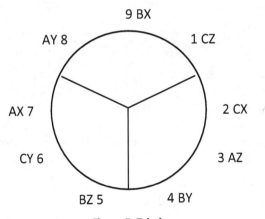

9 BX

AY 8   1 CZ

AX 7   2 CX

CY 6   3 AZ

BZ 5   4 BY

Figure 5: Triads

Formative years

As a child, we need *emotional nurturance* and learn what we *should do* given our circumstances. The parental role is to guide a child towards independence in such a manner they will make sound choices when left to their own resources.

The classic role of the mother (M) is to emotionally nurture, accept, and give the child a sense of self-worth.
The classic role of the father (F) is to provide, protect, and wean the child away from the mother towards independence.
Both provide guidance in their own way and teach us how to cope with the world we live in.

Our role models are typically the biological mother and father. We must also realize the traditional roles can be fulfilled by anyone. For instance, an older sister can be the emotional nurturer or a protector for a younger sibling.

In our formative years, we learn to feel attached (+), frustrated (-), or rejected (~) by one or both role models. This explains why there are nine core perspectives[13], core needs, and consequent behavioral patterns.

+ M (3)	- M (7)	~ M (8)
+ F (6)	- F (1)	~ F (2)
+ M/F (9)	- M/F (4)	~ M/F (5)

The attached (+ 369) fend for themselves (3: I will succeed; 6: I am dutiful; 9: I find peace). The frustrated (- 147) place demands on others (1: embrace my convictions; 4: accept me; 7: help me get what I want). The rejected (~ 258) meet needs of others (2: let me help you; 5: give what you need; 8: protect you).

---

[13] according to the Enneagram

Distinct and consistent

The perspectives evolve and develop into nine distinct and consistent behavioral patterns. The patterns are distinct for a good reason. Behaviors stack like building blocks on top of each other as one thing leads to another. We tend to do what we know best and when we do not get what we want, we exaggerate what we know best.

Development	Behavioral Pattern
Healthy *Manipulation*	1 Integration with others 2 Self-acknowledgment 3 Socially inclusive
Average *Domination*	4 Do what we know best 5 Emphasize core needs 6 Ego-oriented
Unhealthy *Control*	7 Exaggerate what we know best 8 demands core needs to be met 9 Socially exclusive
Disintegration: *Mental illness*	↓ Do the opposite of what we know best. Pathological

A child grows up feeling vulnerable. She learned to protect herself by presenting herself as strong. In duress, exaggerating strength becomes dominance which escalates into dictatorship. She has done what she knows best and is now at the end of her rope. She has been too forceful, too direct, and too blunt. She retreats out of fear for retaliation making her feel vulnerable. This pattern, from confrontation to withdrawal, is distinct, consistent, and predictable.

We also exaggerate verbally in order to *convince others of an untruth*. Lines like "honest to God!", "I swear!", and "I had no idea!" are such lines. For instance, to deny to have no idea means denying an already existing idea. Thus, they had an idea in the first place.

Predictability

We build on our past. What we did yesterday influences what we do tomorrow. In essence, the past has predictable value.

Tomorrow starts today

The present points to our choices in the past. A good analogy is the alphabet. If today is K, then we know LMNO will follow. We also know GHIJ came before it. It is the same in behavioral patterns. The Type Two and Eight patterns show how one thing builds on another.

Two: *I must be good*
- altruistic, inspiring
- helps others[14]
- unwanted help
- confrontational

Eight: *I must protect myself*
- strong, empowering
- domineering
- dictatorial
- withdrawal

We recognize core patterns but everyone but details will differ. Our unique life experiences determine what matters the most.

The best predictor of future behavior is (relevant) past behavior.

- Dr. Phil

Two people with the same pattern will have two very different reasons: *Nancy Grace is a TV talk show host. She is strong, domineering, and interrupts her guests frequently (reactivity). Her fiancée was murdered and she became a lawyer fighting crime. Gordon Ramsey is a chef on TV. He is strong, domineering, even dictatorial, and reactive. He grew up with an alcoholic and abusive father. Both felt vulnerable and both compensated by taking charge. They are the same; it's the details that differ.*

---

[14] Healthy Twos help others without expecting a return (altruism). Average Twos help others and expect love and appreciation in return (masking own neediness).

Dynamic

The Enneagram is a dynamic model where everyone is everything but we emphasize one core need over the other. A good analogy is: "Anybody can use a hammer, but when you use a hammer on a daily basis, you're a carpenter." The combination of behavioral styles, social styles[15], and expression of perspective tends to point in the direction of your type.

Types 378 *(assertive)*, 612 *(dedicated)*, and 945 *(withdrawn)* share how they get what they want.

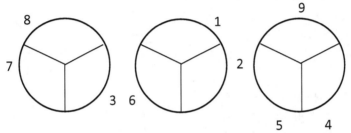

Figure 6: Behavioral Style similarities

Types 315 *(methodical)*, 648 *(demonstrative)*, and 927 *(positive)* share how they present themselves in social settings.

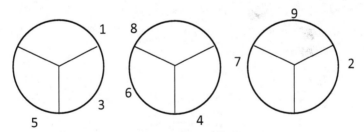

Figure 7: Social Style similarities

---

[15] see perspective test page 34

No pure type

There are many influences on a type and implies at times types are hard to recognize. There are numerous misidentifications possible therefore when you believe you know someone's type, continue to pay attention as you might find a better alternative.

Regardless, no matter what type someone is really does not matter. We are all everything while we emphasize one thing over the other.

They are who they are while knowing someone's type only helps you to understand them better.

The following influences are clearly present:
- similarities in behavioral style
  - 378 assert and insist
  - 612 dedicated and reliable
  - 945 withdrawn and imaginative
- similarities in social style
  - 315 logical and methodical
  - 648 emphatic and demonstrative
  - 927 positive minded and people oriented
- wing
  - type next to your own with the most influence
  - flavors our type
- mental health
  - integration
    - healthy individuals acquire healthy characteristics of the next type in the model
  - disintegration
    - unhealthy individuals acquire unhealthy characteristics of the next type in the model

Behavioral style groups

The behavioral style groups are the first step to recognizing a type. The three types in each group will have strong similarities in behaviors but are motivated by entirely different perspectives.

These groups are akin to Freud's triad: Id, Ego, Super-Ego
- 378: Id oriented. The Id wants immediate gratification. They are the "I want it, I want it now!" types. They have strong desires, are energetic, and industrious (Fight response).
- 612: Super-Ego oriented. The Super-Ego weighs morals and values. "Is this right, wrong, fair, unfair, good, or bad?" They internalize prevailing mores, seek structure, and order (Fear response).
- 945: Ego oriented. The Ego mediates between the Id (impulse) and Super-Ego (impulse control). "I want it, but do I need it?" They withdraw to think, use their imagination to resolve problems, and are identity focused (Flight response).

The similarities in behavior have been described in the perspective test[16] and reflect on the table marked ABC.

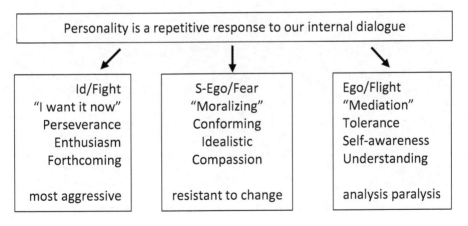

Figure 8: Fear, Fight, Flight responses

---

[16] page 36

Social style groups

The three types in each social style groups have similarities in how they present themselves in social settings. Again, these groups have been described in the perspective test (XYZ).

- 315: we don't show our emotions readily. We keep emotional distance and may come over as aloof.
- 648: we share our emotions readily. We wear our emotions on our sleeve and want others to feel the way we do.
- 927: we don't worry too much. The glass is half full and things will work out anyway.

The combination of behavioral style and social style is the core of our behavioral pattern and identifiable through observation.

The behavioral cluster for type Three is:
- I have a "I want it, and I want it now" attitude
- I assert and insist
- I am logical and methodical

And may be interpreted as:
- → my perspective is success orientation
- → I need performance acknowledgment

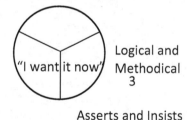

Figure 9: Response, behavioral and social style cluster for Type 3

Wing

The types next to our own type influence our behavior. The type with the most influence or impact on your behavior is called your wing.

This is best explained with an analogy. If your type is olive oil then a garlic infusion flavors the oil. But, you are still oil. A wing flavors your type[17].

The types next to a Three are Two and Four. A Three can be a 3w2 ("Three wing Two") or 3w4.

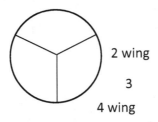

2 wing

3

4 wing

Figure 10: Wing

A Three wants to be seen as a success. Threes, like Sevens and Eights, are assertive and insistent.
A Two is an outgoing people pleaser. Therefore, a 3w2 is an assertive, insistent, success driven individual whose outgoing and extroverted influences adds to their assertive nature.
A Four is an introverted self-aware individual and adds reservation to a Three. A 3w4 is an assertive, insistent, success driven person whose reservation adds to their logical and methodical personality.
And so, 3w2 may be referred to as "the Charmer" and the 3w4 as "the Professional."

---

[17] Donald Trump 3w2 (2 adds outgoing) and Mitt Romney 3w4 (4 adds reserved)

Mental health

There are three major mental health levels[18].
- healthy
- average
- unhealthy

The same type functioning at different levels of mental health can look quite different to us.

Yet, when we recognize the nine distinct patterns, we learn to see through the differences and understand healthy personalities *integrate* others, average types *emphasize* core needs to be met, and unhealthy individuals *demand* core needs to be met.

Integration
A person functioning at healthy mental levels will acquire healthy characteristics of the next type in the integration model. The integration sequence is 1758241 and 3693.

A healthy One will learn to enjoy life like a healthy Seven (1 to 7).
A healthy Seven will gain profound insight like a healthy Five (7 to 5).

Disintegration
An individual functioning at average and unhealthy mental levels will acquire the average and unhealthy traits of the next type in the disintegration model. The disintegration sequence is 1428571 and 3963.

An unhealthy Two will become domineering and destructive like an unhealthy Eight (2 to 8). An unhealthy Eight will withdraw out of fear for retaliation like an unhealthy Five (8 to 5).

---

[18] page 47

Example: 3w2

Every type has influences of many other types supporting the idea that "everybody is everything."

As an example, a Three is assertive and insistent like the Seven and Eight. A Two wing flavors the Three by adding social relatedness. A healthy Three gains the healthy qualities of a Six whereas an average to unhealthy Three acquires the unhealthy traits of a Nine.

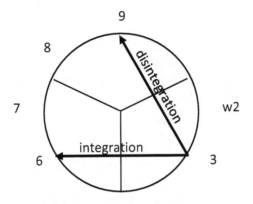

Figure 11: integration - disintegration

As we can see, a Three has the following influences:
- Seven and Eight: add enthusiasm and candor to perserverance
- Two adds social relations to self-promotion
- Six replaces self-promotion with cause commitment
- Nine replaces self-promotions with disengagement

It suffices to say that *"Nobody is a pure Type"* and is the reason why we might not recognize our own type initially. This explains why we may initially misidentify self, a friend, or acquaintance.

It is beyond the scope of this material to further elaborate[19].

---

[19] Please refer to addendum "Main Theme" for some insight in the integration and disintegration model.

Summary

There is a pattern to how we develop:

- we are born with natural abilities
- we are influenced by our environment
- childhood identification with role models
- nine (9) childhood perspectives
    - how we see ourselves
    - how we see the world
    - how we fit in
- core need
- strengths and weaknesses
- behavioral and social style
- information processing
- ego-defense mechanism

We learn to recognize types through behavioral style, social style, and what they say.

Each type has numerous influences:
- each type belong to a group (378, 612, 945)
- flavored by a wing
- Level of mental health
    - acquires healthy qualities (175824 and 369)
    - acquires unhealthy qualities (438571 and 396)

7. What is the Enneagram model about?
8. Why is a behavioral pattern distinct and consistent?
9. What differentiates one Type from the other in a group?
10. What is a Wing?

_____

_____

_____

_____

_____

_____

_____

_____

_____

_____

_____

_____

_____

_____

_____

_____

_____

_____

_____

_____

_____

_____

_____

_____

_____

_____

_____

_____

_____

_____

The model

What we want

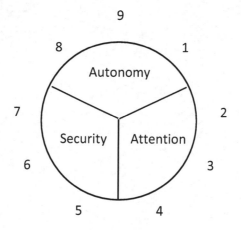

Figure 12: Wants

We all want the same three things in life.
- Attention, or to be appreciated for who we are
    - seeks self-worth
- Security, or to feel safe with the ones we are with
    - seeks to make sense of life
- Autonomy, or to make choices we deem best for us
    - resists reality

The model shows that
- Types 234 emphasize attention seeking behaviors because they don't feel appreciated for who they are
- Types 567 emphasize security seeking behaviors because they don't feel safe with the ones they are with
- Types 891 emphasize autonomy seeking behaviors because they don't feel they can rely on others

Attention Triad

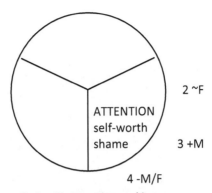

Figure 13: Attention seeking

Types 234 do not feel appreciated for who they are and prone to self-worth and shame issues. They compensate by presenting themselves better than they are with a façade of how they want to be seen. This makes them image oriented and they present themselves as altruistic (2), a success (3), and as unique (4).

Threes are children who felt appreciated and rewarded when they performed well. Their feelings were minimized and not adequately addressed. They linked self-esteem to performance and learn to present themselves as "a Success." Three's key need is to feel *worthy, valuable, and to be seen as a success*.

Twos are children who only felt loved when they helped others first. They link self-esteem to being good to others and present themselves as "Altruists." Two's key need is *unconditional love, to be loved, and to be appreciated for what they do for you*.

Fours are children who felt others have something they do not. They are different and feel excluded. They link their self-esteem to being different and present themselves as unique. Four's key need is to *fit in, to be included, to find what is missing*.

Security Triad

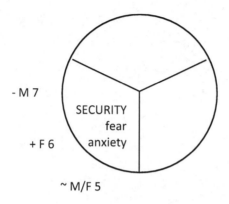

Figure 14: Security seeking

Types 567 do not feel safe with the ones they are with and are prone to fears and anxieties. They compensate by displacing their anxiety by focusing on something else instead of confronting it.

Sixes are children who grew up with self-doubt, didn't know what to do, and didn't know who to turn to. Their self-esteem is linked to doing what others think is best or they become authority defiant. Six's key need is to *have your support, to figure out what to do, and need your help to decide.*

Fives are children who did not feel acknowledged and their emotional needs were not important to others. They were without meaningful nurturance and guidance or may have felt defenseless against intrusions. They compensate by trying to understand the world to feel safe. The Five's key need is to be seen *as intelligent, competent, and informed.*

Sevens are children who felt deprived of emotional nurturance. They compensate by finding nurturance themselves and link self-esteem to insisting in getting what they want. They reduce anxiety by being preoccupied in activities and become busy bees. The Seven's key need is *to stay preoccupied and get what they want now.*

Autonomy Triad

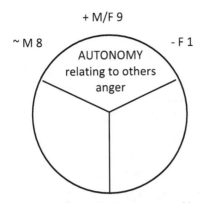

Figure 15: Autonomy seeking

Types 891 do not feel they can rely on others and are prone to having difficulties relating to others and anger. They compensate by becoming self-reliant and suppressing their anger.

Eights are children growing up in an unsafe environment. Their weakness was exploited making them feel vulnerable. They learn to self-protect by presenting themselves as strong and make sure they are not seen as weak. Eight's key need is to feel safe by *being in charge and self-reliant*.

Nines are children growing up feeling neglected, not listened to, and unimportant. When they expressed their needs, like anger, they were ignored or put down for having needs. They learn to not speak up, keep the peace, and tolerate others instead. Nine's key need is *to be heard, keep the peace, and maintain support*.

Ones grew up with heavy criticism and felt the rules they had to abide by were inconsistent, poor, flawed, or plain wrong. They learn to focus on doint better and improving existing rules. They set their own standards often more rigid than the ones provided. One's key need is *to improve the world by setting personal standards*.

Behavioral Styles

Sigmund Freud introduced a psychological Triad:
- Id: needs immediate gratification
    - *"I want it, I want it now"*
    - *irrational, no reflection on consequences*
- Super-Ego : mediates between ideals and conscience
    - *"Is this good, bad, right, wrong, fair, unfair?"*
    - *standards of right and wrong*
- Ego: mediates between ideals and reality
    - *"I want it, but do I need it"*
    - *standards of real versus imagined*

There are three core responses in how we get what we want:
- Fight (378)
- Fear (612)
- Flight (945).

Figure 16: Freud and core responses

Assertives

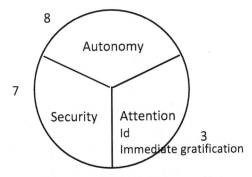

Figure 17: The Assertives 378 (Id / fight response)

Types 378 received an imbalance in *emotional nurturance*. They compensate by getting what they want themselves. They are assertive, insistent, and do not let others bother them. They are preoccupied obtaining their goals and disregard anyone threatening their objectives.

- 3 seeks Attention or to be appreciated
- 7 seeks Security or to feel safe with the ones they're with
- 8 seeks Autonomy or to be self-reliant

They are prone to *overstep boundaries* without realizing the emotional impact they have on others.

Assertives 378 (tend to overstep boundaries)
- self-esteem comes from within
- they insist on getting what they want
- see themselves in positive light allowing assertion
- direct and action oriented approach to personal needs
- Three demands attention
    - *I get attention by inspiring others to my success*
- Seven demands security
    - *I feel safe when preoccupied in activities*
- Eight demands autonomy
    - *I feel self-reliant when in charge*

Dedicated

Figure 18: The Dedicated 612 (Super-Ego / fear response)

Types 612 have an imbalance knowing what to do or *guidance*. They do what they believe is expected from them and tend to be moralizing. They feel good when adhering to existing principles. They ignore contradictory evidence to maintain emotional balance. They are dedicated to rules and reliable to follow through with them.

- 6 seeks Security or to feel safe with the ones they're with
- 1 seeks Autonomy or to be self-reliant
- 2 seeks Attention or to be appreciated

They are prone to *emotional reactivity* without realizing they can be highly irrational.

Dedicated 612 (tend to over-react)
- self-esteem is conditional on conviction approval
- see themselves positively when abiding by their convictions
- attempt to earn what they need
- present themselves as moralizers
- 6 earns security
    - *I feel safe by conforming to rules*
- 1 earns autonomy
    - *I feel self-reliant by setting my own standards*
- 2 earns attention
    - *I get attention by being good first*

Withdrawn

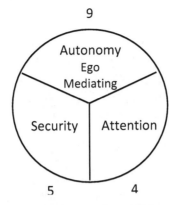

Figure 19: The Withdrawn 945 (Ego / flight response)

Types 945 grew up with an imbalance in acknowledgement. They tend to be reserved and like to be alone. They come over as passive since they do not come into action readily. They solve problems through thinking and are compelled to investigate. They withdraw to think and use their imagination to solve problems.

- 9 seeks Autonomy or to be self-reliant
- 4 seeks Attention or to be appreciated
- 5 seeks Security or to feel safe with the ones they're with

They are prone to *overthinking, procrastination,* and do not realize imagined action is not a real solution.

Withdrawn 945 (tend to over-think)
- self-esteem depends on approval from others
- don't see themselves in a positive light
- withdraw to think
- disengage to deal with own needs
- 9 withdraws to gain autonomy
  - *I feel self-reliant creating my private space*
- 4 withdraws for attention
  - *I get attention by lamenting and withdrawal*
- 5 withdraws for security
  - *I feel safe observing from a distance*

65

Compliant - Defiant

Each response group (378, 612, 945) consists of a primary type in the center of a triad (369) and two secondary types in the opposite position of the primary type (3-78, 6-12, 9-45). This provides each response group type with a different emphasis on a core want: autonomy, attention, and security.

The secondary types are a compliant and defiant behavioral version of the primary type.

Assertives

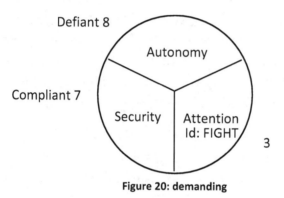

Figure 20: demanding

Types 378 *demand* attention (3), security (7), and autonomy (8).

3 is compliant demanding attention
3 is defiant by demanding compliance

7 is compliant demanding security by taking care of themselves
8 is defiant demanding autonomy by having others do as they say

They are Freud's Id oriented types with a Fight response. We see them as "*demanding.*" Types 378 are self-oriented, assert and insist on personal wants and needs. They may be charismatic and woo others to cooperate. They tend to be action-oriented and forceful.

Dedicated

Figure 21: moralizing

Types 612 *earn* security (6), autonomy (1), and attention (2).

6 is compliant earning security doing what others think is best
6 is defiant earning security by questioning what is best

1 is defiant earning autonomy by setting personal standards
2 is compliant earning attention by adapting to others

They are Freud's Super-Ego oriented types with a Fear response. We perceive them as "*moralizing*." Types 612 focus on values, traditions, and customs of society. They don't like to veer away from prevailing mores, question progress, insist on existing principles, and enforce personal standards.

Withdrawn

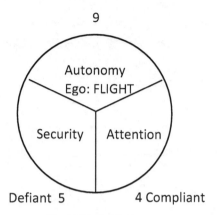

Figure 22: mediating

Types 945 seek approval and obtain autonomy (9), attention (4), and security (5) by keeping their distance.

9 is compliant seeking autonomy by being amicable and agreeable
9 is defiant seeking autonomy by passively resisting others

4 is compliant seeking attention by keeping to themselves
5 is defiant seeking security through abstract understanding.

They are Freud's Ego oriented types with a Flight response. We interpret them as *"mediating"* and passive. They tend to keep their emotional distance, are pre-occupied in thought, and tend to stay in the background. They tend to have answers to questions others haven't asked themselves yet.

Social Styles

Methodical

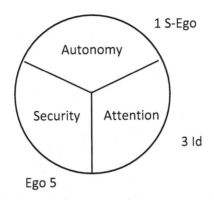

Figure 23: Logical and Methodical

Types 315 tend to control themselves and are not comfortable sharing their feelings. They keep their emotional distance and may even come over as aloof. They are *logical* and *methodical*.

The model maps these clusters for each type
Type 1 is
- autonomy seeking
- Super-Ego orientation (moralizing)
- dedicated and reliable
- logical and methodical

Type 3 is
- attention seeking
- Id orientation (gratification)
- assertive and insistent
- logical and methodical

Type 5 is
- security seeking
- Ego orientation (mediating)
- withdrawn and imaginative
- logical and methodical

Demonstrative

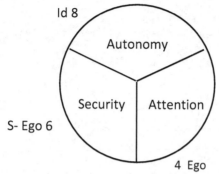

Figure 24: Emphatic and Demonstrative

Types 648 wear their emotions on their sleeves. They readily share them with others and want others to feel the way they do. They are *emphatic* and *demonstrative*.

The model maps these clusters for each type
Type 4 is
- attention seeking
- Ego orientation (mediating)
- withdrawn and imaginative
- emphatic and demonstrative

Type 6 is
- security seeking
- Super-Ego orientation (moralizing)
- dedicated and reliable
- emphatic and demonstrative

Type 8 is
- autonomy seeking
- Id orientation (gratification)
- assertive and insistent
- emphatic and demonstrative

Positive

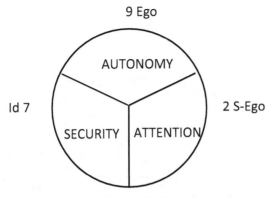

Figure 25: Positive Minded and People Oriented

Types 927 tend to be enthusiastic about life. They like people and see a glass as half full. They believe things will work out anyway, so why worry? They are *positive minded* and *people oriented*.

The model maps these clusters for each type
Type 7 is
- security seeking
- Id orientation (gratification)
- assertive and insistent
- positive minded and people oriented

Type 9 is
- autonomy seeking
- Ego orientation (mediating)
- withdrawn and imaginative
- positive minded and people oriented

Type 2 is
- attention seeking
- Super-Ego orientation (moralizing)
- dedicated and reliable
- positive minded and people oriented

11. What do we all want?
12. How do we get what we want?
13. How do we present ourselves?
14. How do we recognize types?

Information processes

This chapter delves into how we process information. It helps to explain why we misunderstand each other.

We operate from different perspectives and have a unique combination of experiences. It turns out, we also process information very differently and it seems we speak a "different language."

We have three ways we process information. They are
- Head
- Heart
- Gut (Body)

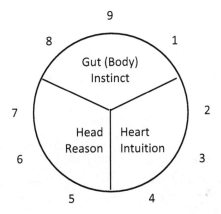

Figure 26: Processing Centers

The Head center

The head center reflects on our reality and wisdom. Observation and reasoning to keep us safe by anticipating the world. The common emotions of the head center are fear and anxiety.

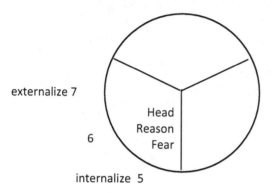

Figure 29: Head center

Types 567 are the Head Types and focus on being safe (Security). They go about finding security in quite different ways:

- 6: the Six reacts to fear by imagining worst case scenarios leading to self-doubt. They prepare themselves for when things go wrong and seek guidance outside themselves.
- 5: the Five reacts to fear by retreating into thought and minimizing personal needs. They observe the world from a distance and analyze situations.
- 7: the Seven react to fear by turning discomfort into excitement to avoid feelings of fear and anxiety. They become busy bees and are experience oriented.

We see 567 as *Objective.* Five internalizes reality, Six represses reality, and Seven engages with reality.

The Heart center

The heart center reflects on our intuitive life. Our emotions, how we see ourselves or our identity, and how we relate to others. It provides us with self-worth, meaning, and why we exist. This is why the number one need is to be appreciated for who we are.

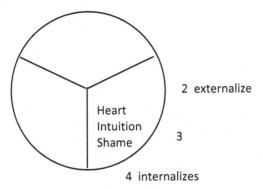

Figure 28: Heart center

Types 234 are the Heart Types and seek recognition and validation (Attention). When we don't receive the attention we need, we feel deficient, shame, and worthless. This is why the number one fear is rejection. Types 234 go about getting attention in quite different ways:

- 3: the Three is most out of touch with their emotions. They link self-worth to accomplishments and present themselves with an image of success to ward off shame.
- 2: the Two externalizes their feelings by being good to others. They present themselves likeable, good, and altruistic. They seek positive regard from others to ward off shame.
- 4: The Four internalizes their emotions in search for their identity or the reasons why they are different and unique. They dramatize their hurts through withdrawal, moodiness, and shame avoidance.

We see types 234 as *Subjective*. Two externalizes emotion, Three represses emotions, and Four internalizes emotions.

The Gut center

The gut or body center reflects on our instinctual life force, vitality and our physical presence in the world. Our presence must be protected and anger springs into action for survival.

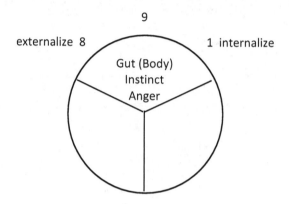

Figure 27: Gut center

Types 891 are the Gut (Body) Types and are focused on seeking to be self-reliant (Autonomy). They go about finding independence in quite different ways:

- 9: the Nine is most out of touch with instinctive gut reactions. They disconnect from anger, avoid conflict, and do not confront whatever threatens their inner peace.
- 1: the One represses and internalizes their anger presenting them self as cordial and friendly. They hold back their instinctive impulses leading to pent up anger.
- 8: the Eight readily expresses their anger through confrontation. They guard themselves through dominance to ward off others.

We see types 891 as *Reactive*. Eight externalizes their reactions, Nine represses reactions, and One internalizes reactions.

Intelligence Centers

In sum, we have three intelligence centers available to us.

For simplicity reasons, I refer to them as
- THINK ~ Objective, reasoning, conscious thought
- FEEL ~ Subjective, emotions, intuition
- DO ~ Reactive, instinct, gut reactions

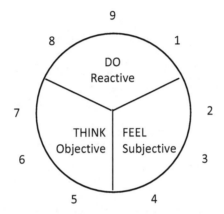

Figure 30: Intelligence or processing Centers

The intelligence centers should be equally employed but, as we will now find out, each type tends to have one dominant center, a supporting center, and a repressed center[20].

- the dominant center is used first and foremost
- the supportive center supports the dominant center
- the repressed center is employed last and least

---

[20] Kathleen Hurley inspired

Reactive and Objective

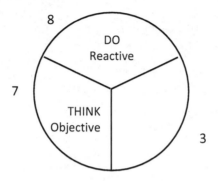

Figure 31: DO and THINK

Types 378 experienced some form of emotional abandonment in their childhood like "you were an accident" or "parental separation because of drugs." Their ability to feel love underdeveloped. They learn to repress emotions, and reject emotional connectedness to others (≠FEEL). Their challenge is to open up emotionally and make themselves vulnerable in intimate relationships.

What is left for them is to come readily into action (DO+THINK). Types 378 are self-assertive, competitive, and spontaneous with an "I want it now!" (Id) attitude. They tend to not understand the emotional impact they have on others and overstep social boundaries with relative ease. Types 7w8 and 8w7 are the most aggressive types.

Each type emphasizes one processing center supported by their secondary center.

	Dominant center	Supporting center
3	Objective	Reactive
or 3	Reactive	Objective
7	Objective	Reactive
8	Reactive	Objective

This is the core of "the one percent."

Reactive and Subjective

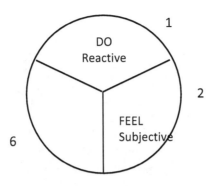

Figure 32: DO and FEEL

Types 612 were provided some form of unreliable information. They deemed information not trustworthy. This may be verbal and non-verbal contradictions like "The beating is for your own good". They reject their perception of reality and under develop reasoning leading to strong personal, and often rigid convictions (≠ THINK).

What is left for them is emotional reactivity (FEEL+DO). Types 612 are conforming, idealistic, and compassionate with a moralizing attitude (Super-Ego). They internalize prevailing morals and values and prone to emotional over-reactivity. Types 1w2 and 2w1 are the most resistant to change.

Each type emphasizes one processing center which is supported by their secondary center.

	Dominant center	Supporting center
6	Reactive	Subjective
or 6	Subjective	Reactive
1	Reactive	Subjective
2	Subjective	Reactive

This is the core of conservatism.

79

Objective and Subjective

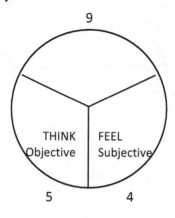

Figure 33: THINK and FEEL

Types 945 experienced rejection, feeling unwanted, or not acknowledged. This may be due to detached and cold parents. They do not believe in themselves and feel they don't make a difference the world (≠DO).

What is left for them is to reason their emotions (THINK+FEEL). Types 945 are self-aware, tolerant, and need understanding with an "I want it but do I need it?" attitude (Ego). They internalize their position in the world, how to fit in, and prone to procrastination. Types 4w5 and 5w4 are the most withdrawn types.

Each type emphasizes one processing center which is supported by their secondary center.

	Dominant center	Supporting center
9	Objective	Subjective
or 9	Subjective	Objective
4	Subjective	Objective
5	Objective	Subjective

This is the core of the progressives.

Relationship dynamics

It is fairly easy to understand others when we see why they behave the way they do. We often don't because we don't see their *intent*.

Figure 34: Intent

The following exchange took place in a billiards hall. A garrulous type 3w2 plays pool. He is an average player overstating his abilities attempting impossible shots.

One: *"I can't stand that guy. He puffs himself up. He is arrogant and likes you to believe he is great but he isn't!"* Notice how the One is critical and judgmental.
Five: *"We all have our quirks. Yours is anger."* Notice the true versus not true filter.
One: *"Really?"* [He just threw a cue ball through the pool hall.]
Five: *"Yes, we all have our baggage. You need to understand where others are coming from. He is puffing himself up because he is compensating for not being that good. His self-esteem depends on playing well. He does not control the cue ball, loses frequently, and that makes him feel worthless. That is why he pretends to be better than he really is. It's a façade to make himself feel better."*

For me personally, to understand intent reduces the impact of how others behave. Yes, he is arrogant. So what? He is making himself feel better.

81

15. What are the three processing centers?
16. Why is this important to realize?

_____
_____
_____
_____
_____
_____
_____
_____
_____
_____
_____
_____
_____
_____
_____
_____
_____
_____
_____
_____
_____
_____
_____
_____
_____
_____
_____
_____

In sum

Nobody is a pure type
There are nine core perspectives
There are nine distinct behavioral patterns

We want three things
- attention
- security
- autonomy

There are three core responses or behavioral styles
- assertive and insistent (Fight: Assertives)
- dedicated and reliable (Fear: Moralizing)
- withdrawn and imaginative (Flight: Mediators)

There are three ways we present ourselves or social styles
- logical and methodical
- emphatic and demonstrative
- positive minded and people oriented

There are three processing centers
- Head (reasoning, objectivity, THINK)
- Heart (emotions, subjectivity, FEEL)
- Gut (action oriented, reactivity, DO)

Explore the patterns in the models and familiarize yourself with the behavioral clusters for each type.

17. Summarize what you have learned and why this is important

Identifying types

Each Type belongs in a behavioral style group. They share behaviors based on their core response or "how we *get* what we *want*."

Type identification is easiest by first focusing on the main core response (fear, fight, flight) and then focus on a more distinct habitual pattern within the group.

Freud outlined how we *get* what we *want*:
- Id wants immediate gratification
  - We assert ourselves (Fight response)
    - Get what we want
    - Confront others
    - Persevere
- Super-Ego wants to weigh morals and values
  - We feel good adhering to convictions (Fear response)
    - Enforcing personal standards
    - Compassionate to others
    - Conforming to authority
- Ego wants to mediate between the Id and Super-Ego or impulse versus impulse control
  - We seek acknowledgment and approval from others (Flight response)
    - Aware and self-aware
    - Listen to others
    - Abstract understanding

Each Type manipulates to get what they want and are prone to a speaking style. They focus on their core perspective and reveal themselves by what and how they talk about it.

How to recognize a type

We can recognize groups by their core habitual responses (fear, fight, flight). That is a good start. Each group shares similarities in behavioral styles and how they express themselves. However, each type will emphasize their own core perspective. A Three woos others with "how great I am." A Seven is lengthy and Eight confrontational.

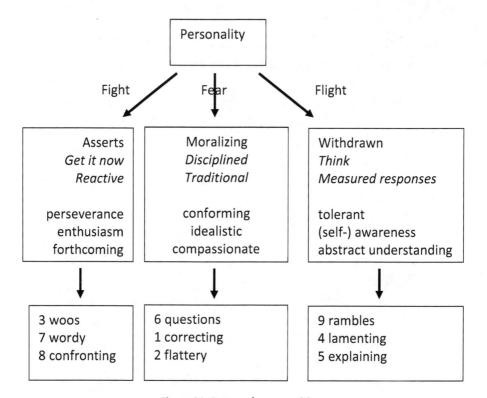

Figure 31: Pattern for recognition

Who doesn't know Donald Trump? He is a type Three (3). He asserts himself, is highly reactive saying things he did not think through properly. He is self-promoting, wooing others about "how great he is." He talks through others with lengthy (7) and confrontational (8) messages. He is a Three because his core perspective is self-promotion, stating "it is all about success", yet, clearly shares behavioral characteristics with Seven and Eight.

86

How each Type manipulates

Assertives

3	Charms others	Tells what you want to hear
7	Distracts others	Insists on getting needs met
8	Dominates others	Demands to do as they say

Dedicated

6	Complains	Tests other's commitment
1	Corrects others	Insists on their standards
2	Helps others	Makes self needed

Withdrawn

9	Disengages	Passively resists others
4	Moodiness	Makes others walk on eggshells
5	Thought preoccupation	Creates emotional distance

Speaking Styles

Assertives

3	Charms others	Woos and inspires others
7	Distracts others	Scattered story lines
8	Dominates others	Challenges whose in charge

Dedicated

6	Complains	Questions everything and warns
1	Corrects others	Instructs and moralizes
2	Helps others	Flattery and advisory role

Withdrawn

9	Checks out	Rambles monotonously
4	Moodiness	Laments and self-pity
5	Thought preoccupation	Systematic explanations

Recognizing 378

Assertive and insistent (Fight response)

The Id oriented triad (378) grow up with their emotional needs inadequately addressed and learn to seek immediate gratification. They assert themselves and insist on getting what they want. They are industrious, assertive, and insistent. They become competitive, confrontational, and spontaneous. They are self-oriented and typically don't let others bother them or get in their way.

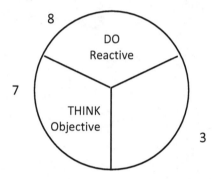

Figure 35: Assertive and Insistent

The Assertives typically do not acknowledge failure, limitations, nor admit to the emotional impact they have on others. They are prone to overstepping boundaries without realizing they do. They see themselves as charming, empowering, and fun but others may get the impression they are being used and just along for the ride.

The Assertives have many behavioral characteristics in common, but what sets them apart is their core perspective or the reason why they behave this way.

- 3: I must be seen as a success
- 7: I must stay pre-occupied in activities
- 8: I must be in charge

Type Three "the Opportunist"[21]

- grows up feeling appreciated only when they excel
- THINK: "I am not worthy unless I succeed"
- FEEL: "I must succeed"
- DO: work hard and strive to excel
- fear: to be worthless
- need: to have value
- strengths: perseverance, spontaneity, candor
- tend to not admit to failure, limitations, emotional impact

- Healthy: ambitious
- Average: competitive
- Unhealthy: exploitative

I grew up feeling loved and appreciated only when I performed well. The core of Type Three is to present themselves as worthy. They focus on gaining admiration in order to boost self-worth and to feel valuable. Threes believe others need praise and admiration like they do. They are hardworking, energetic, and optimistic. They learn to strive for success, become ambitious, competitive and work-a-holics.

Their strength is Perseverance. A need to win at all cost may lead to exploitation.

Their Vice is Deceit, or presenting themselves better than they really are. They are prone to overstating their abilities and grandiosity.

Their Ego Defense Mechanism[22] is Identification or acting as if they are like you. They tell you what you want to hear so you like and help them get what they want. They also use rationalization and denial.

Type Three improves by shedding the idea value is dependent on positive feedback from others. When a Three is self-assured and self-

---

[21] See addendum "Main themes" for type summaries.
[22] see Ego Defense Mechanisms in addendums

affirming, they will learn to focus on commitment to causes instead of personal success.

At insecure levels, denied and despised, they may become vindictive and, in the end, completely disengage.

Type 3	Vice: Deceit *(overstating abilities)*
Perspective	I don't feel worthy unless I succeed Failure is not an option
Fear	I fear not being able to live up to my inflated self-image
Need	I earn admiration through performance acknowledgment
Filter	"Am I seen as a success?"
Perspective	I must excel I must be better than you I must be seen as a success
Ignores	Preoccupied with representing themselves as a success, they will not admit defeat or failure
Flaw	Excessive need for finding worth leads to chasing success and win at all cost.
Typical conflict	Others feel exploited by their narcissism. Arrogance, condescension, and contempt leads to confrontation
Creating my own fears	*Others reject me because of my arrogance, exploitation. Now I am truly worthless and emotionally empty*

What we think
- why am I treated with disrespect for my abilities?
- I don't understand why they change the rules midway
- I don't understand why they are not as committed as I am

What we say
A Type Three typically makes statements involving how good they are seeking performance acknowledgment
- my mother appreciated and supported me
- I am a momma's boy
- I work hard and play hard
- I achieve because I go for it
- Nothing can stop me
- White lies are just fine
- I am a Type A personality
- I want things and I want them now
- I am admirable
- I am desirable
- I am a winner
- I am the best
- I don't let emotions get in the way
- I never had close friends
- What others think is not important to me

Type Seven "the Optimist"

- grows up without significant emotional nurturance
- THINK: "I feel deprived"
- FEEL: "I lack emotional nurturance"
- DO: I stay pre-occupied in activities (busy bee)
- fear: missing out
- need: fulfillment
- strengths: spontaneity, perseverance, candor
- tend to not see limitations, failure, and emotional impact

- Healthy: satisfied
- Average: acquisitive
- Unhealthy: insatiable

I grew up feeling I had to take of care myself as I did not rely on others. I am always looking for "what is next", with a "more is better" attitude. The core of Type Seven is experience oriented.
They are high energy, entertaining, and limitless. They typically have conflict over lack of follow through and exaggerated promises.
They do not want their children to feel deprived like they were and may give their children what they want.

Their strength is coming into immediate action or Spontaneity. Over-involvement in too many activities leads to hyperactivity without appreciating any of them. They spread themselves thin.

Their Vice is Gluttony or overdoing things. They tend to start something new and exciting before the previous task has been finished. Over-involvement in too many tasks eventually becomes overwhelming and they break down.

Their Ego Defense Mechanism is Rationalization or putting positive spins to negatives negating reasons for not coming into action. They also use denial and identification.

The vivacious and enthusiastic Seven may learn to appreciate what they have and limit activity involvement. The insecure Seven may become over-involved in too many activities, becomes scattered in their thinking, and then critical and judgmental.

Type 7	Vice: Gluttony *(overdoing things)*
Perspective	I feel deprived You did not take care of me
Fear	I fear deprivation; fear of missing out
Need	I want to have freedom and happiness
Filter	"What can I do next?"
Perspective	I must have pleasant new experiences Find self-gratification Stay pre-occupied in activities
Ignores	Personal limitations
Flaw	From seeking happiness to being overwhelmed (involved in too many commitments)
Typical conflict	Impulsivity and superficiality leads to unfulfilled promises
Creating my own fears	*Immediate gratification does not bring happiness after all making me feel deprived*

What we think
- You have no right to limit or restrain me
- I can justify my wrong doing
- I think negatively of you when I am hurt

What we say
A Type Seven typically makes statements involving excitement.
- Mother wasn't really available for my needs
- I get what I want because nobody else will
- I want to have fun!
- I get bored easily
- I love doing things with people
- There is always room for more
- I have many, many friends, but not close friends
- I plan my day and change plans on a whim

Type Eight: "the Authoritarian"

- grows up feeling their weakness was exploited
- THINK: "I must be self-reliant"
- FEEL: "I am vulnerable"
- DO: I focus on being forceful
- fear: others will harm me
- need: to be strong and dominant
- strengths: candor, perseverance, spontaneity
- tend to not see their emotional impact, failure, and limitations.

- Healthy: Strong
- Average: Domineering
- Unhealthy: Dictatorial

I grew up in an unsafe environment and my weaknesses were exploited. I must never show I feel vulnerable or weak. I learned to focus on being self-reliant and strong. I will take charge and present myself with an "I will get you before you can get to me" attitude. The core of Type Eight is self-protection. They present themselves larger than life and fill a room. They tend to protect those who are vulnerable and exploited. Type Eight vouches for the "underdog."

Their strength is Candor and in excess becomes directness and bluntness.

Their Vice is Lust for power. They might become domineering and overwhelming. They are prone to megalomania.

Their Ego Defense Mechanism is Denial or denying the existence of negatives while enforcing their opinions. They also use rationalization and identification.

Healthy Eights are strong, empowering, and have compassion for others becoming the true leaders they can be. At unhealthy levels, they can be blunt, ruthless, and dictatorial.

Type 8	Vice: Lust *(for power)*
Perspective	I am exploited I feel vulnerable
Fear	I fear others will harm, hurt me
Need	To be self-reliant, to be in charge
Filter	"Will I be harmed?"
Perspective	I protect myself I am going to get you before you get me
Ignores	Emotional impact on others
Flaw	Self-protection develops into constant fighting
Typical conflict	Misplaced over-confidence leads to unacceptable behaviors like ruthless bullying, directness, and bluntness.
Creating my own fears	*Destruction of others leads to retaliation. Now I am at the mercy of others making me feel vulnerable*

What we think

- I put you down when you don't live up to your potential
- I have negative thoughts when things do not manifest
- I feel outrage when no t in control

What we say

A Type Eight typically makes statements involving power and control.

- I am stronger than you
- I have to protect myself and the underdog, who else will?
- You are with me or get out of the way
- I have leadership abilities
- I am empowering
- Emotions make you weak
- I like confrontation and tell others off
- I can be direct and blunt
- I have an "in your face" attitude

Assertive and Insistent Do's and Don't's

Each Type wants to be appreciated for who they are and need confirmation for how they see themselves. Here are guidelines for interactions with Types 378.

The Assertive and Insistents We get what we want now We are reactive and reasoners			
Filter	Intent	Do	Don't
3 The Opportunist			
Do you see me as a success?	I make things happen	Tell me you admire me Be direct, clear, concise Love me for what I do	Be overly emotional Point out my failures Interrupt me when I am working
7 The Optimist			
What to do next?	I want to have fun	Have fun with me Enjoy my spontaneity Appreciate my grand visions	Be clingy or needy Micromanage me Ask me about details
8 The Authoritist			
Who will hurt me?	I protect myself by taking charge	Stand up for yourself Be direct and strong Share your vulnerability	Take my challenge personally Betray my trust Put me in a box

18. What do the Assertives have in common?
19. What is the core perspective of a Three?
20. What is the core perspective of a Seven?
21. What is the core perspective of an Eight?

_____

_____

_____

_____

_____

_____

_____

_____

_____

_____

_____

_____

_____

_____

_____

_____

_____

_____

_____

_____

_____

_____

_____

_____

_____

_____

_____

_____

_____

Recognizing 612

Dedicated and Reliable (Fear response)

The Super-Ego triad (612) grows up with guidance inadequately addressed. Guidance is your path toward independent and appropriate decision making. They mediate between ideals and conscience. They weigh morals and values and ask themselves "is this right, wrong, good, bad, fair, or unfair?" They want to be good, do right, and be supportive. They tend to adhere to their convictions and like others to embrace their beliefs. They are moralizing, conforming, and compassionate. They are prone to emotional over reactivity.

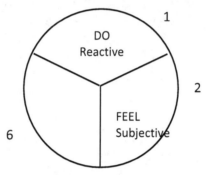

Figure 36: Dedicated and Reliable

The Dedicated typically do not see they may become blindly obedient, may not see gray areas, and may repress personal needs. They see themselves as conforming, having integrity, and kind-hearted but others may experience them as rigid in opinions, overstate their views with an air of superiority, and providing unwanted assistance.

Again, the reason why they act this way, or their core perspective, sets them apart:

- 6: I doubt myself
- 1: I must improve the world
- 2: I must be good to others

Type 6: "the Conformist"

- grows up with self-doubt
- THINK: "I don't know what to do and who to turn to"
- FEEL: "I want support and decision assistance"
- DO: I will do what you think is best
- fear: loss of support
- need: support and guidance
- strengths: loyalty, fairness, empathy
- tend to not see blind obedience, gray areas, and personal needs.

- Healthy: Self-guiding
- Average: Dutiful
- Unhealthy: Obedient

I grew up in an uncertain environment creating self-doubt and had no one to turn to. I learned to rely on what others thought was best.
I can be compliant and do what others think is best. I am also defiant as I need to show I am independent. They are generally loyal, responsible, and dedicated. Typically, their constant questioning and testing support frustrates others and may drive them away.
Type Six as parents may provide their children with strong guidance removing the self-doubt they have. They feel good adhering to their convictions which may be authority dependent or defiantly independent.

Conviction adherence naturally develops Loyalty and excess loyalty may lead to blind obedience[23] or not questioning the input from others.

Their Vice is Fear for loss of support and guidance. They are prone feeling inferior and testing others' support.

---

[23] I suspect this is the basis for the "Stockholm syndrome"

Their Ego Defense Mechanism is Projection or applying personal traits to others. They also use reaction formation and repression.

A healthy Six learns to trust their judgment and becomes self-guiding. An unhealthy Six is a worrywart, indecisive, and chronically ambivalent.

Type 6	Vice: Fear *(for loss of support)*
Perspective	I don't trust my own judgment I question everything
Fear	I fear being abandoned and alone
Need	I want security through guidance and reassurance of support
Filter	"Do I have your support?"
Perspective	I must do what others expect of me Do what others think is best
Ignores	Authority fallibility
Flaw	Overestimating quality of support leads to blind obedience
Typical conflict	Self-doubt leads to questioning everything frustrating others
Creating my own fears	*My insecurity, anxiety, and inner conflict drive others away, and now I am without guidance, support, and alone*

What we think
- Why are you negative towards me?
- I worry about what can go wrong all the time
- I doubt myself, feel dependent, but want to be independent

What we say
A Type Six typically makes statements involving morals and values.
- I always relied on my father, my best friend, and confidante
- I am careful to be responsible
- I want to know the rules and find the boundaries
- I am skeptical, ask many questions, and confuse myself
- I don't really trust people and I don't know what to do

Type One: "the Idealist"

- grows up with heavy criticism and/or strict discipline
- THINK: "nothing is ever good enough"
- FEEL: "I am not good enough."
- DO: Strives to improve self and the world.
- fear: being flawed, bad, corrupt, amoral
- need: to be moral, good, diligent, prudent
- strengths: fairness, loyalty, empathy
- tend to not see gray areas, blind obedience, acknowledging personal needs

- Healthy: Prudent
- Average: Idealistic
- Unhealthy: Rigid

I grew up with guidance I perceived as inconsistent and flawed. I tend to believe you had no meaningful guidance either. The core of Type One is to provide others with guidance. They are formal, prudent, and generally well mannered, yet, conflict is typically about who is right.

Their strength is Idealism. Rigidity in principles may lead to enforcing personal standards with emphatic certainty.

Their Vice is Wrath, or explosive anger outbursts towards others not trying as hard as they do. They are prone to self-righteousness.

Their Ego Defense Mechanism is Reaction Formation. They replace an undesirable response with the opposite. For instance, acting extra nice to someone they dislike which leads to pent-up anger. They also use repression and projection.

A healthy One learns to enjoy life and sheds the pursuit of perfectionism. An unhealthy One retreats with guilt, remorse, and torments self after yet another explosive tirade.

Type 1	Vice: Wrath *(others don't try as hard as I do)*
Perspective	I am not good enough I am self-critical
Fear	I fear not being good enough, amoral, and being condemned
Need	To improve the world
Perspective	I must be better I must improve the world I strive for perfection
Filter	"Is this right or wrong?"
Ignores	Gray areas
Flaw	Enforcing personal standards with emphatic certainty
Typical conflict	Others are angered by constant judgment and criticism
Creating my own fears	*Rigidly adhering to my convictions and telling others what to do gives me disapproval and condemnation instead*

What we think
- I judge right from wrong, good from bad, fair from unfair
- I mostly focus on what is wrong and keep mental notes
- I question people's integrity when they do wrong

What we say
A Type One typically makes statements involving perfectionism.
- My father expected me to be better all the time
- My father blamed me for everything
- I constantly walked on eggshells
- I know right from wrong[24]
- Things can always be better and improve
- I have higher standards and try harder than anybody else
- I am prudent and reasonable
- That is not what I taught you

---

[24] Dr. Phil asked a "One guest": When is the last time you made a mistake? The 50-ish year old male answered famously: "When I was seven."

Type Two "the Altruist"

- grows up feeling unloved
- THINK: "I am not worthy of love"
- FEEL: "I must earn love and appreciation"
- DO: Always being good to others
- fear: to be without unconditional love
- need: to be loved and appreciated
- strengths: empathy, loyalty, fairness
- tend to ignore personal needs, may be blindly obedient, and does not acknowledge gray areas.

- Healthy: Altruistic
- Average: Good intentions
- Unhealthy: Providing unwanted help

I grew up feeling unloved and I link my self-esteem to being good to others. The core of Type Two is to give others love and appreciation. They are warm-hearted and flirtatious. Problems arise when people feel favored only to find out they were not. They often feel under-appreciated for their efforts. They may become overinvolved and make themselves needed.

Their natural strength is Compassion. Over-involvement and excessive need for reciprocation may lead to histrionics and pay back demands.

Their Vice is Pride in being needed. They will go to great lengths to meet others' needs while forgetting their own. They may become sanctimonious or act as hypochondriacs for attention.

Their Ego Defense Mechanism is Repression or not acknowledging personal needs. They also use projection and reaction formation.

Type Two improves by shedding the idea others need them and learn to attend to their own needs first. A healthy Two is altruistic, compassionate, and inspiring. An unhealthy Two, severely disappointed with lack of return for all their efforts, becomes domineering and may even resort to violence against intimates.

Type 2	Vice: Pride *(in being needed)*
Perspective	I am unloved
	I put other's needs before mine
Fear	I fear not being loved
Need	To be loved and appreciated
Perspective	I must earn love and appreciation
Filter	"Will I be loved?"
Ignores	Personal needs
Flaw	Makes self needed even when not wanted
Typical conflict	People think they are favored but are not
Creating my own fears	*My unwanted advice and good deeds drive others away and now I am not loved*

What we think

- I worry about doing things for others without reciprocation
- Why don't you listen to the advice I give you
- Why do people treat each other with ill will?

What we say

A Type Two typically makes statements involving love.

- I love my dad but he didn't notice me
- I know I am good
- I give, give, give
- I am a people pleaser
- I love others more than I love myself
- I go out of my way to be nice
- I like to help
- It feels good to be needed
- Love solves all problems
- I am the best friend you can wish for

Dedicated and Reliable Do's and Don't's

Each Type wants to be appreciated for who they are and need confirmation for how they see themselves. Here are guidelines for interactions with Types 612.

Filter	Intent	Do	Don't
The Dedicated and Reliables We abide by our convictions We are emotional and reactive			
6 The Conformist			
Do I have your support?	I conform or defy existing rules	Set clear expectations Reassure me of your support Help me decide	Overreact when I do Let me down Be ambivalent
1 The Idealist			
Is this good, right, or fair?	I want to improve things	Tell me I am prudent Ask for my advice Help me enjoy life	Let me do all the work Question my integrity Tell me I am irresponsible
2 The Altruist			
Do you love me?	I get you what you need	Appreciate my efforts Ask me about myself Let me know you care	Take me for granted Be indifferent, detached, cold Make me feel left out

22. What do the Dedicated have in common?
23. What is the core perspective of a Six?
24. What is the core perspective of a One?
25. What is the core perspective of a Two?

_____

_____

_____

_____

_____

_____

_____

_____

_____

_____

_____

_____

_____

_____

_____

_____

_____

_____

_____

_____

_____

_____

_____

_____

_____

Recognizing 945

Withdrawn and Imaginative (Flight response)

The Ego triad (945) grow up with their emotional needs and guidance inadequately addressed. They had no meaningful interaction with their role models, were left to their own resources, and feel unacknowledged and don't fit in. They learn to withdraw and use their imagination to solve problems. They stay out of the limelight, keep their emotional distance, and tend to come over as passive. They are self-aware, tolerant, and insightful.

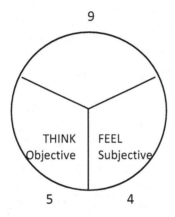

Figure 37: Withdrawn and Imaginative

The Withdrawns tend to not express their opinions, won't acknowledge personal strengths, and do not see that what is readily available to them. They see themselves as easy-going, insightful, and original in thought.

The motivation behind these behavioral characteristics identifies each type:

- 9: I must keep the peace
- 4: I must find inclusion
- 5: I must understand

Type Nine "the Passivist"

- grows up feeling unimportant and not listened to
- THINK: "I must keep the peace"
- FEEL: "I need to avoid conflict"
- DO: I am amicable and agreeable
- fear: loss of connection, abandonment
- need: peace, space, time
- strengths: tolerance, discernment, originality
- tend to not express personal preferences

- Healthy: Peaceful
- Average: Tolerant
- Unhealthy: Complacent

I grew up feeling unimportant and not listened to. My opinion was not important and I learned to keep quiet. Why put effort in when nobody listens? They learn to walk away, roll their eyes, and think "whatever" while disagreeing. The core of Type Nine is to keep the peace by not expressing their personal preferences. They appear unflappable and act with indifference. Conflict arises when their general passive-aggressive tendencies escalate to hysteria.

Their strength is Tolerance and in excess becomes passivity and/or complacency.

Their Vice is Sloth, or passively resisting others. They are prone to self-abandonment and literally "disappear."

Their Ego Defense Mechanism is Narcotization or engaging in mind numbing repetitive tasks. They also use isolation and introjection.

A confident Nine learns their opinion is important enough and expresses their preferences. An insecure Nine might become hysterical and demands to be heard. This is now counter-productive.

Type 9	Vice: Sloth *(Indolence)*
Perspective	I don't matter I am not important enough
Fear	I fear loss of support and separation
Need	I want harmony and peace
Perspective	I must be amicable, agreeable
Filter	"Can I tolerate this?"
Ignores	Expressing personal preferences
Flaw	From keeping the peace to stubbornly neglectful
Typical conflict	Passivity leaves others in the dark not knowing what to think
Creating my own fears	*Passivity leads to disengagement and now I am alone and abandoned*

What we think

- They don't listen to me, why bother to effect change
- People need to be more open-minded and tolerant
- I am too nice and taken advantage off

What we say

A Type Nine typically makes statements involving indecision, non-commitment, and passivity.

- My parents are nice
- I am not that important
- I don't get upset easily
- Accept them the way they are
- It's a waste of time to try to change things
- It's easier to go with the flow
- I am easy-going
- Everyone has the right to their opinion
- I do whatever they want to do

Type Four "the Individualist"

- grows up feeling different and excluded
- THINK: "I am flawed and different"
- FEEL: "I must find personal significance"
- DO: I must find what is missing
- fear: to be insignificant
- need: to be unique and significant
- strengths: originality, tolerance, discernment
- tend to not acknowledge their own strengths

- Healthy: Inspiring
- Average: Moody
- Unhealthy: Self-absorbed

I grew up not identifying with either role model. I always felt different and excluded. The core of Type Four is to find what makes them feel flawed or what is "missing." Their appearance ranges from nothing ordinary to downright bizarre. Typical conflicts arise from their emotional unavailability.

They learn to self-reflect and search for personal identity. Their strength is Self-awareness. Becoming overly self-conscious may lead to emotional self-torment and self-loathing.

Their Vice is Envy, or coveting what others have. Yet, once they obtain what others have, they are disappointed and start looking for what else is missing leading to chronic disappointment.

Their Ego Defense Mechanism is Introjection or applying negative environmental aspects to themselves. They also use isolation and narcotization.

Type Four improves by shedding the idea others have it better. They can inspire others when they embrace personal qualities. An unhealthy Four drowns in dark thoughts and self-loathing.

Type 4	Vice: Envy *(Coveting what others have)*
Perspective	I don't fit in I feel excluded
Fear	I fear being without an identity
Need	I want to be accepted for who I am
Perspective	I am different
Filter	"They don't understand me"
Ignores	Personal strengths
Flaw	Chronic disappointment
Typical conflict	Internalizes hurts without expressing solutions or finding resolve
Creating my own fears	*Keeping my distance and being different ensures I don't fit in and now I am excluded*

What we think

- What is wrong with me? Others?
- Why do they have what I don't?
- Reality always falls short from what I expected

What we say

A Type Four typically makes statements involving melancholy.

- My parents weren't really interested in me
- The more I looked at myself, the less I liked me
- I am a bit of a loner
- I feel alone
- I feel excluded
- I feel unloved
- I feel misunderstood
- I feel others should help me
- I think about death at times
- My childhood wasn't a happy one
- I don't feel good

Fours want to be included and passively wait for others to include them. They are introverted, imaginative, and want others to "rescue" them. They are prone to like super-heroes, a rescuer substitute. Watch for tattoos, t-shirts, belt buckles etc.

Type Five "the Realist"
- grows up feeling unacknowledged
- THINK: "the world is unreliable"
- FEEL: "my needs are not important to you"
- DO: information junkies, sit back and observe
- fear: being useless, incompetent
- need: to be competent, in the know
- strengths: discernment, originality, tolerance
- tend to not see what is right in front of them

- Healthy: Insightful
- Average: Knowledgeable
- Unhealthy: Intellectually arrogant

I grew up in an environment without meaningful interaction with my role models, could not rely on them giving me a "the world is unreliable" perspective. My needs were not important and I do not want you to feel the same. The core of Type Five is to be "in the know" and meet your needs by offering specialized knowledge. They learn to observe, gather information, and keep emotional distance. Their strength is Discernment. Over-thinking may lead to useless over-specialization and social isolation. Type Five feels easily intruded upon and time is their most valuable asset. Their dress code is ordinary and unassuming.

When a Five has good understanding of a subject, they become confident with a strong need to share what they found out. An insecure Five becomes scattered in their thinking and acts out their fears irrationally. They become paranoid out of fear for not understanding the world and not knowing what comes next.

Their Vice is Avarice, or retention of knowledge and expertise. They tend to keep to themselves to use information later. They are prone to intellectual arrogance.

Their Ego Defense Mechanism is Isolation or time to think. They also use narcotization and introjection.

Type 5	Vice: Knowledge hoarding *(Secrecy)*
Perspective	I don't feel acknowledged my needs are not important to you
Fear	I don't feel safe in the world I fear being helpless, useless I fear being inadequate, incompetent
Need	I want to understand the world I want you to listen to what I figured out
Filter	"Is it true or not true?"
Perspective	I want to understand To be competent To have knowledge
Ignores	Preoccupied in thought, does not pay much attention to what's right in front of them
Flaw	Excess knowledge turns into useless over-specialization
Typical conflict	Retreats into thought and emotionally unavailable
Creating my own fears	*Being unavailable and alone, now I am helpless and useless*

What we think

- People are aggressive and intrusive
- I anticipate what others are going to do
- What gives you the right to interrupt what I am doing?

What we say

A Type Five typically makes statements involving knowledge.

- My parents are okay but were cold and distant
- I am a loner, inquisitive, and observant
- I keep my distance to avoid obligations
- Knowledge is power and I like predictability
- I don't want to intrude
- I love to share what I have learned

Withdrawn and Imaginative Do's and Don't's

Each Type wants to be appreciated for who they are and need confirmation for how they see themselves. Here are guidelines for interactions with Types 945.

The Withdrawn and Imaginatives We observe and think We are reasoners and emotional			
Filter	Intent	Do	Don't
9 The Passivist			
Is this tolerable	I keep the peace	Listen to what I say Be patient with me Hug me	Make me hurry Be confrontational Take advantage of my passivity
4 The Individualist			
Do you understand me?	I want to be included	Appreciate me for who I am Share your feelings Accept my intuition	Be rude, direct, and blunt Hide behind a mask, wall Tell me to get over it
5 The Realist			
Is it true or not true	I want the facts, the truth	Be independent Be consistent in sharing your thoughts Be warm but not sappy	Intrude or expect immediacy Be demanding Rush me

26. What do the Withdrawns have in common?
27. What is the core perspective of a Nine?
28. What is the core perspective of a Four?
29. What is the core perspective of a Five?

Strengths

We repeat what we know best. Repetition develops into a strength. Observe others and learn from their strengths.

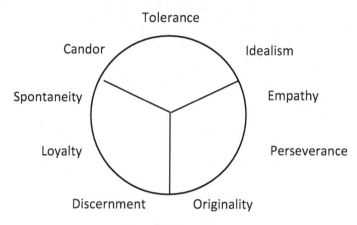

Figure 38: Strengths

The groups 378, 612, and 945 share their strengths and each type owns a personal strength. Of course, anyone can be tolerant but Nines are the most tolerant as they need to avoid conflict to maintain their connection with others. This principle applies to all types.

	Core behavior	Strength developed
3	Become successful	Perseverance
7	Enjoy new experiences	Spontaneity
8	Confrontational	Candor

6	Conviction adherence	Loyalty
1	Improve the world	Idealism
2	Earn love	Compassion

9	Keep the peace	Tolerance
4	Find personal identity	Originality
5	Abstract understanding	Discernment

Blind spot

We meet our core need to maintain our self-image and self-worth. We meet these needs through choice, behaviors, and repeat what we know best. Experience and repetition make us good at what we do. However, when we try too hard, our strength develops into a weakness.

Excess strength becomes a weakness

In our, now excessive, quest to meet our core need, we may not see or acknowledge we are driven by a core fear. We deny who we are by giving in to our fears and not meeting our core need. This negatively impacts our self-image and self-worth. This is a form of self-deception and develops into a blind spot.

The Assertives

The Assertives focus on personal needs, assert, and insist on getting what they want. They undervalue emotions and underdevelop their ability for emotional intimacy in relationships.

	Core need	Strength	Blind spot
3	I must succeed	Perserverance	Failure
7	I must stay active	Spontaneity	Limitations
8	I must be in charge	Candor	Emotional impact

Type Three feels they must succeed. They come into action, work hard, and won't stop until they succeed. Their strength becomes "perseverance." When they need to succeed, or win, at all cost, they may do so over the back of others. Perseverance becomes exploitation as the Three will not accept "failure."

Type Seven feels they must be involved in activities. They come into action and in their enthusiasm start a new task before the first is finished. Their strength becomes "spontaneity." When they spread themselves thin by being involved in too many activities, spontaneity develops into scattered hyperactivity as they will not accept their "limitations."

Type Eight feels they must be in charge. They challenge others to figure out who is in charge and develop candor as their strength. They will say things with social disregard and become too direct and too forthcoming. Candor develops into bluntness as they do not consider the "emotional impact" they have on others.

The Dedicated

The Dedicated internalize prevailing morals and values, are dedicated to maintaining rules, and reliable to follow through. They undervalue information accuracy and underdevelop personal judgment.

	Core need	Strength	Blind spot
6	I must conform	Loyalty	Blind obedience
1	I must do better	Idealism	Gray areas
2	I meet your needs	Compassion	Personal needs

Type Six feels they must conform to prevailing conventions and seek to do what they believe is expected. They typically look for guidance from those they believe are in the know, an authority if you will. Their strength becomes "loyalty." Loyalty develops into "blind obedience" when they accept authority guidance without personal consideration.

Type One feels they must do better and improve the world. They must figure out the right way to do things and correct themselves and others. They develop a sense of right versus wrong and "idealism" is their strength. With such a black and white perspective, they will not acknowledge "gray areas."

Type Two is preoccupied with the needs of others and become self-forgetting regarding "personal needs." In their zest to assist others, they may make themselves needed and even provide "unwanted assistance."

The Withdrawns

The Withdrawns focus on their position in the world, withdraw to think, and need to figure out how to fit in. They undervalue themselves and underdevelop the belief they make a difference in the world.

	Core need	Strength	Blind spot
9	I must have peace	Tolerance	Personal preferences
4	I must be included	Originality	Personal strengths
5	I must understand	Discernment	Useless over-specialization

Type Nine must have tranquility and find their peace through conflict avoidance. They learn to be non-confrontational by not expressing what their wants and need. Their amicable and agreeable attitude develops into "tolerance." Tolerance develops into "complacency" when conflict is avoided at all cost.

Type Four feels different and excluded. They believe others have something they don't. They compensate by presenting themselves as having something others don't and become "original." In their quest for a personal and original identity, they may get "stuck" in a never ending "emotional loop." They are forgetful about their "personal strengths" while focusing on the strengths of others.

Type Five must have understanding. They are inquisitive and search for abstract truth which leads to their strength "discernment." In their quest to understand, they may overdo their search and want to know anything and everything developing into "useless over-specialization."

In sum, our blind spot is self deceiving and a defense mechanism to maintain our self-image and self-worth.

Weaknesses

Observe others, recognzine weaknesses, and influence with compassion.

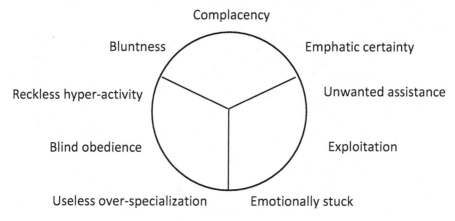

Figure 39: Excess strength

The groups 378, 612, and 945 share their weaknesses and emphasize their own above the other two. Any type can provide unwanted advice but type Two, who needs to earn appreciation, is predisposed to make themselves needed.

	Develops strength	Excess strength becomes weakness
3	Persevere	Win at all cost or exploitation
7	Spontaneity	Scattered hyper-activity
8	Candor	Lack of filter leads to bluntness

6	Loyalty	Blind obedience
1	Idealism	Rigid emphatic certainty
2	Compassion	Unwanted assistance

9	Tolerance	Passivity leads to complacency
4	Self-awareness	Emotionally repetitive thoughts
5	Discernment	Knowing too much becomes useless

Typical Conflicts

The Assertives

The *Assertive* 378 come into action and justify their choice afterwards. They typically get into trouble because they overstep social boundaries and do not understand the emotional impact they have on others.

The ambitious and competitive Three avoids losing status, failure, and being over-shadowed by others. They tend to overstate their abilities. They make exaggerated promises they can not be keep. Conflict arises when others interfere with their progress or they do not deliver. Their tools to fight back are *arrogance* and *condescension*.

The enthusiastic "what's next" Seven avoids boredom, limitations, and frustrations. They get over-involved in too many commitments they cannot keep. They become *scattered, skip commitments*, and do not finish tasks already started.

The self-protective Eight avoids being seen as weak, indecisive, and dependent. They need to be strong and respected. They are forthcoming and can become *blunt*, direct, and *"in your face."* Their confrontational attitude may develop into constant fighting.

The Dedicated

The *Dedicated* 612 are emotionally reactive. They tend to be moralizing, weighing right, wrong, good, bad, fair, and unfair. Their typical conflict is based on telling others what they should do without considering the perspective of others. They set the rules, want others to embrace their convictions, and effectively remove others' choices.

The self-doubting Six avoids being dependent and gets stuck in doubt, contrary thoughts, and indecision. They test your support, question everything, and frustrate others with *chronic ambivalence.* They are hard to please with ever changing plans and outcomes.

121

The principled Type One avoids making mistakes, losing control, and integrity. They are moral gatekeepers with standards of right and wrong. They may become rigid in their opinions. Their anger comes in sudden explosive outbursts where they *enforce* their *personal standards* with emphatic certainty, even when dead wrong.

The people-pleasing Two avoids disappointing others, feeling unloved, and under appreciated. They are warm hearted, well-intentioned with big hugs and smiles. Twos get into trouble as they feel they give, and give, and feel others do not reciprocate. Twos typically *hint* at their needs which others do not see. The may retaliate and become violent and destructive.

The Withdrawns

The *Withdrawn* 945 (over-)think before they speak. They mediate between wants and needs. Their typical conflict is about being emotionally distant and physically unavailable.

The agreeable Nine avoids conflict, confrontation, and discomfort. They tend to not express their opinions and walk away with too many demands on them. The problem with not expressing an opinion is the other person will *not know where the Nine stands* and means others cannot address their needs.

The quiet individualistic Four avoids exclusion, the mundane, and insignificance. They are preoccupied in thought and tend to wait for others to engage with them. They have unequaled emotional depth and seem *not approachable, distant*, and *unavailable*.

The inquisitive Five avoids intrusions, demands on their time, and incompetence. They are easily overwhelmed in new environments. They do not like small talk and wander from one conversation to the next in search of something valuable to hear or say. They keep their *emotional distance*, may come over as distant, and *aloof*.

Boundaries

Life happens and gets to us now and then. We may overreact and say things we regret later. Sometimes we meet people who rub us consistently wrong. This is frequently based on differences in core perspectives, core needs, and how we process information.

Fives tend to know what they are doing as they research subject matter extensively. Ones tend to tell others what they should do. A Five thinks "I know already" and the One believes "they are helping others to improve things." In this case, the One repeated the same unwanted advice for weeks. The Five is now frustrated with the One and interprets the One as intrusive, annoying, and self-righteous. Yet, the One sees himself as helpful.

If you don't have boundaries,
I will set them for you.

The Five made clear he was not interested through non-verbals and telling the One: "I know already. Thank you, that is nothing new." The One continued to pursue his own need to make thing better or improve the world providing unwanted advice.
The Five, now frustrated, tells the One: "I had enough of your advice. You are one of the most self-righteous individuals I ever met." The core belief system of a One is to be right and to be called self-righteous was offensive. He quit providing unwanted advice.

We teach others how to treat us.

We all have certain needs and views on life. We give others a permission slip to continue to step over boundaries unless we tell them not to. We can do that in anger or tell them the opposite of what they need to hear.

Give

Our behavior constantly shifts around fulfillment of our core need. We repeat our behaviors because this is what we know best. From our perspective, we tend to believe others have similar needs. Therefore,

we give others what we need the most.

Type Four feels excluded. They include others.
Type Eight feels vulnerable. They protect the vulnerable.
Type Nine feels not listened to. They listen to others.

	Thought	Destiny
	Assertives "gratification"	
3	I want to be praised	I praise you
7	I want to get what I want	I get you what you want
8	I want to protect myself	I will protect you
	Dedicated "moralizing"	
6	I want your support	I support prevailing values
1	I want to do better	I help you do better
2	I want to be loved	I love you
	Withdrawn "mediating"	
9	I want to be listened to	I will listen to you
4	I want to be included	I will include you
5	I want my needs acknowledged	I acknowledge your needs

What we want to hear

Each type has a core need they *need* to hear confirmed to feel validated. Our wing provides the second most important need we *like* to hear. We also *want* to hear what the other two types in our group (378, 612, 945) want to hear.

How do we figure out what someone wants to hear the most?
We start by recognizing the three core response groups. We know each group contains three types and as a group each type likes to hear all three compliments. Each type, however, *needs* to hear their personal need the most.

The big picture groups are fairly easy to recognize and using all three needs will sit well with the recipient. In the meantime, observe which one they respond to the strongest. It will take time to establish a noticeable pattern.

Assertive and Insistent Types (FIGHT response)
We get what we want and insist getting it now ("action oriented")   3. to hear I am good at what I am doing (praise)   7. to hear you support me getting what I want (acquisition)   8. to hear you keep me safe (security)
Dedicated and Reliable Types (FEAR response)
We focus on following rules of society ("morality")   6. to hear you support me and help me decide (guidance/support)   1. to hear I am prudent and moral (decency)   2. to hear I am loved and appreciated (altruism)
Withdrawn and Imaginative Types (FLIGHT response)
We think before we speak ("thoughtfulness")   9. to hear you listen to my opinion (importance)   4. to hear you include me (inclusiveness)   5. to hear you listen to what I learned (teaching)

It will take more time to identify a specific Type and wing through behavioral style and what people say. Experience will guide you to become proficient.

To reiterate what we need to hear the most
- Type = *needs* to hear
- Wing = *likes* to hear
- group = *wants* to hear

A Type 3w2, first and foremost, *needs* to hear they are very good at what they do. The next thing they *like* to hear is they are loved (2). Lastly, they *want* to hear they are safe and have your assistance.

3	That I am good, even excel, at what I am doing
2	That I am loved and appreciated for being good
7	That you support me getting what I want
8	That I am safe and okay

A Type 3w4 also wants to hear they are very good at what they do. However, the Four wing has a different need than the Two wing.

3	That I am good, even excel, at what I am doing
4	That I am included and accepted for who I am
7	That you support me getting what I want
8	That I am safe and okay

Each Type - Wing has their own combination of what they want to hear[25]. They share the needs according to the 378, 612, and 945 groups.

---

[25] see addendum "What we want to hear"

Alliances and cooperation

It is abundantly clear we need to meet the needs of others to gain friendships. This applies to parents, teachers, businesses, and life. Anyone in a leadership position needs to gain the trust of those they lead and need to make them want to cooperate and do better.

It is imperative to allow others to be who they are and have a positive influence by standing beside them. We can always gently nudge them into a better direction if there is one. Those who feel appreciated will work harder to not lose their most valuable asset: YOU.

**To be appreciated for whom we are
is the most powerful compliment we can receive.**

Life is simple when we have a clear vision of what we want and need to do. It is the purpose in our lives.

Consider these "rules of engagement"[26]:
- appreciate others → provides self-worth (attention)
- be supportive → a place to fall (security)
- allow choice → sense of self-reliance (autonomy)
- be positive → allows to move forward
- think before you speak → encourages measured responses
- be excited → encourages success

I suggest everyone, parents and teachers especially, to think about:
1. Have a clear vision
    a. With a clear vision comes clarity of expectations
    b. Chronic ambivalence gives a child the feeling they are unable to please; it sets them up for disappointment and see themselves as a failure

---

[26] Attention, Security, Autonomy, Positive Minded and People Oriented, Withdrawn and Imaginative, Emphatic and Demonstrative.

2. Build confidence
    a. Expectations need consistency
    b. We can support and re-direct building self-esteem leading to cooperation
    c. To punish and shame leads to resentment
3. Let them be who they are
    a. This is where the nine perspectives come in handy
        i. I need to be seen as prudent, objective
        ii. I need to be loved and appreciated
        iii. I need to succeed
        iv. I need to be appreciated for who I am
        v. I need to be seen as informed, intelligent
        vi. I need your support and advise
        vii. I need you to help me get what I want
        viii. I need you to make me feel safe
        ix. I need you to listen to my opinions
    b. Feed the core needs and give them self-worth
4. Encourage expression of their point of view
    a. There is nothing better than to be appreciated for who you are
    b. Appreciation of choice builds self-esteem
    c. Creates confidence in making solid future choices
    d. Breeds self-reliance
5. Be consistently positive
    a. Put positive spins on negatives and move forward
    b. Don't sweat the small stuff
6. Think before you speak
    a. Words are powerful and hurts may go unnoticed
    b. Tone down; reactivity is often regretted later
    c. Reprimands must be in proportion to the offense
7. Be excited for others
    a. Enjoy their accomplishments with them
    b. Success breeds success and repeats itself

Summary

We explored nine core perspectives and their distinct behavioral patterns to satisfy a core need.

Each Type has a wing and is part of a behavioral group leading to more than one need. Nevertheless, one need is our core need.

We can identify core needs by observing behaviors and listening to what people say. We can make others feel good about themselves by addressing their needs. Our reward is friendship, an alliance, and cooperation.

And so, we have come to conclude:

Life is simple

We give others what we need the most
→ *give them what they give others*

We want to be appreciated for who we are
→ *confirm how they see themselves*

We need to feel safe
→ *set clear and consistent expectations, be honest, and fair.*

Follow your passion
Be inclusive
Be responsible

Pay attention.
Your happiness and success depends on it.

30. What are the core strengths of each Type?
31. What is a weakness?
32. What are the core weaknesses of each Type?
33. What is an Ego Defense Mechanism?
34. What is the concept behind "we give what we need the most?"

_____

_____

_____

_____

_____

_____

_____

_____

_____

_____

_____

_____

_____

_____

_____

_____

_____

_____

_____

_____

_____

_____

_____

_____

_____

_____

Addendums

Test results

The tests are meant to give you some direction to what you may relate to the most. Perspective determines your type and shows through your behaviors. More accurate tests can be found online[27].

You selected two letters according to their significance to you. The combination of these paragraphs (ABC, XYZ) point in the direction of your possible type.

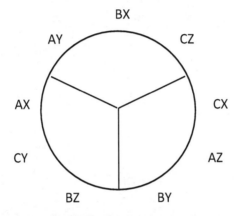

Figure 40: Letters corresponding to type numbers

A: perseverance, spontaneity, candor
B: tolerance, original, discernment
C: loyalty, idealistic, compassion

X: optimistic, engaging, no worries
Y: demonstrative, sensitive, shares feelings
Z: keeps distance, in background, aloof

---

[27] Visit www.enneagraminstitute.com

Word selection

Each type is prone to select a group of words reflecting on their perspective.

		Sees self as
1	CZ	Prudent, objective, realistic
2	CX	Loving, caring, giving
3	AZ	Admirable, desirable, charming
4	BY	Gentle, unique, different
5	BZ	Intelligent, insightful, competent
6	CY	Responsible, trustworthy, dependable
7	AX	Spontaneous, confident, busy bee
8	AY	Empowering, strong, forth-coming
9	BX	Independent, humble, forgiving

Remember, each Type is part of a behavioral style group and has a wing. For instance, a 5w6 relates most to

type

5	BZ	Intelligent, insightful, competent

and relates to a *wing*

6	CY	Responsible, trustworthy, dependable

and relates to *group 945*

9	BX	Independent, humble, forgiving
4	BY	Gentle, unique, different

Groups 378, 612, 945

		Assertives *"gratification"*
3	AZ	I need to succeed and may win at all cost
7	AX	I am a busy bee and may over-do things
8	AY	I am authoritative and may be dictatorial

Types 378 share behavioral characteristics and each type emphasize their own personality traits. They do not let others bother them and are more prone to overstepping boundaries than the other types. They self-assert, persevere, and are spontaneous.

		Dedicated *"moralizing"*
6	CY	I am dutiful and may blindly follow rules
1	CZ	I want to improve things and may be rigid
2	CX	I am good to others and make myself needed

Types 612 share behavioral characteristics and each type emphasize their own personality traits. They are moralizing and are prone to emotional over-reactivity. They are loyal, idealistic, and compassionate.

		Withdrawns *"mediating"*
9	BX	I am agreeable and may be complacent
4	BY	I am unique and may self-torment
5	BZ	I am in the know and may isolate myself

Types 945 share behavioral characteristics and each type emphasize their own personality traits. They (over-) think before they speak and are prone to procrastination. They are tolerant, original, and insightful.

Validation

Meet the core needs of others and gain friendships.
To deny a core need is to deny the person and leads to *resentment*.

	Wants to be seen as	Wants others to
3	Admirable, desirable, charming	How good they are at a task *Tell them they are great*
7	Spontaneous, confident, go-getter	Assist them to get what they want *Help them to accomplish*
8	Empowering, strong, forth-coming	Let them be in the lead *Make them feel safe, in charge*

6	Responsible, trustworthy, dependable	Support them and help decide *Be patient with their self-doubt*
1	Prudent, objective, realistic	Tell them they're correct *Support their opinion*
2	Loving, caring, giving	Love them unconditionally *Loves people and hugs*

9	Independent, humble, forgiving	Be heard, listened to *Ask them for their opinions*
4	Gentle, unique, to be included	Embrace their being *Share what you have*
5	Profound, insightful, competent	Listen to their know how *Listen to their solutions*

What we want to hear

Our needs determine what we need to hear the most. Our wing and group (378, 612, 945) determines what we like to hear.

A wing B

A	Type *(needs to hear)*
B	Wing *(likes to hear)*
C	Other type in your behavioral style group *(wants to hear)*
D	Other type in your behavioral style group *(wants to hear)*

1w9

1	That I am prudent and rational
9	That I am heard and listened to
6	That I am supported and have you help me decide
2	That I am loved and appreciated for being good

1w2

1	That I am prudent and rational
2	That I am loved and appreciated for being good
6	That I am supported and have you help me decide

2w1

2	That I am loved and appreciated for being good
1	That I am prudent and rational
6	That I am supported and have you help me decide

2w3

2	That I am loved and appreciated for being good
3	That I am good, even excel, at what I am doing
6	That I am supported and have you help me decide
1	That I am prudent and rational

3w2

3	That I am good, even excel, at what I am doing
2	That I am loved and appreciated for being good
7	That you support me get what I want
8	That I am safe and okay

3w4

3	That I am good, even excel, at what I am doing
4	That I am included and accepted for who I am
7	That you support me get what I want
8	That I am safe and okay

4w3

4	That I am included and accepted for who I am
3	That I am good, even excel, at what I am doing
9	That I am heard and listened to
5	That you listen to what I have learned

4w5

4	That I am included and accepted for who I am
5	That you listen to what I have learned
9	That I am heard and listened to

5w4

5	That you listen to what I have learned
4	That I am included and accepted for who I am
9	That I am heard and listened to

5w6

5	That you listen to what I have learned
6	That I am supported and have you help me decide
9	That I am heard and listened to
4	That I am included and accepted for who I am

6w5

6	That I am supported and have you help me decide
5	That you listen to what I have learned
1	That I am prudent and rational
2	That I am loved and appreciated for being good

6w7

6	That I am supported and have you help me decide
7	That you support me get what I want
1	That I am prudent and rational
2	That I am loved and appreciated for being good

7w6

7	That you support me get what I want
6	That I am supported and have you help me decide
3	That I am good, even excel, at what I am doing
8	That I am safe and okay

7w8

7	That you support me get what I want
8	That I am safe and okay
3	That I am good, even excel, at what I am doing

8w7

8	That I am safe and okay
7	That you support me get what I want
3	That I am good, even excel, at what I am doing

8w9

8	That I am safe and okay
9	That I am heard and listened to
3	That I am good, even excel, at what I am doing
7	That you support me get what I want

9w8

9	That I am heard and listened to
8	That I am safe and okay
4	That I am included and accepted for who I am
5	That you listen to what I have learned

9w1

9	That I am heard and listened to
1	That I am prudent and rational
4	That I am included and accepted for who I am
5	That you listen to what I have learned

Ego Defense Mechanisms

Ego Defense Mechanisms are strategies used when confronted with conflict and stress. Each Type favors a defense mechanism and shares according to the 378, 612, and 945 groups and their wing.

3	Identification: Presents image of success while feeling like a disappointment Stress reaction *arrogance, contempt, condescension*
7	Rationalization: Presents image of happiness while feeling anxious Stress reaction *hyper-activity, scatterdness, recklessness*
8	Denial: Presents image of strength while feeling vulnerable Stress reaction *dominance, overconfidence, ruthless*

6	Projection: Presents image of loyalty by doing what is expected Stress reaction *dutiful, blind obedience, self-doubt*
1	Reaction Formation: Presents amicable image suppressing inner anger Stress reaction *anger, impatience, emphatic certainty*
2	Repression: Presents as an altruist masking own neediness. Stress reaction *clinginess, over-involvement, hypochondria*

9	Narcotization: Presents image of harmony while feeling conflict Stress reaction *passivity, neglectful, disengaged*
4	Introjection: Presents image of being different while feeling insignificant Stress reaction *moodiness, irrationality, emotional self-torment*
5	Isolation: Presents image of a realist feeling empty and incompetent Stress reaction *detachment, isolation, intellectual arrogance*

Typical conflict

We see ourselves in a certain light and present ourselves accordingly. We must meet our core need and in the end, behavioral exaggeration leads to a typical conflict.

A Type Six grew up with self-doubt and didn't know who to turn to resulting in fears and anxieties over "what to do?" Their self-doubt turns into questioning everything. Not knowing what to do leads to changing their minds ending in chronic ambivalence. This seems innocent enough, however, it is frustrating to others to be constantly questioned and having to meet ever changing expectations.

	Presents self as	Typical conflict
	Assertives	
3	Ambitious, successful, hard-working	Others feel exploited in hindsight
7	Optimistic, limitless, entertaining	Exaggerated promises without follow through
8	Forthcoming, direct, fills room	Throwing their weight around, bullying
	Dedicated	
6	Responsible, trustworthy, reliable	Indecisive, questions every-thing, chronic ambivalence
1	Prudent, formal, well-mannered	About who is right, enforced with emphatic certainty.
2	Warm-hearted, ingratiating, loving	Others feel favored but are not
	Withdrawn	
9	Amicable, agreeable, unflappable	Passive aggressive resistance, complacent, disengaged
4	Different, unique, at times bizarre	Being unavailable, moody, emotionally distant
5	Knowledge focused, intelligent, inquisitive	Emotional distance, aloof, disappears

Main themes

Three: "Do you see me as a winner?"

Threes seek personal value and want to be seen as a success (Attention). They assert, insist, and want immediate gratification. They persevere to succeed and may exploit others. They under value emotions (≠ FEEL) and under develop intimacy in relationships.

Main theme Type 3	
Fear	I am not worthy unless I succeed
Need	I need performance acknowledgment and be seen as a success
Focus	I work hard to succeed
Strength	I learn to Persevere
Weakness	Winning at all cost and willingness to exploit others
Blindness	Not willing to acknowledge failure
Vice	Deceit, or overstating true abilities
Growth	Shed the idea your value is dependent on positive regard
Own friend	Embrace failure as a learning experience
Donald Trump, Mitt Romney, Halle Berry, Lance Armstrong, Michael Jordan	

Healthy Threes become committed to causes (6) whereas unhealthy Threes become passive and disengaged (9).

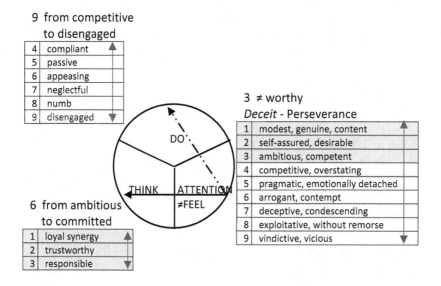

9 from competitive to disengaged

4	compliant
5	passive
6	appeasing
7	neglectful
8	numb
9	disengaged

3 ≠ worthy
Deceit - Perseverance

1	modest, genuine, content
2	self-assured, desirable
3	ambitious, competent
4	competitive, overstating
5	pragmatic, emotionally detached
6	arrogant, contempt
7	deceptive, condescending
8	exploitative, without remorse
9	vindictive, vicious

6 from ambitious to committed

1	loyal synergy
2	trustworthy
3	responsible

Seven: "What is next?"

Sevens seek to make sense of the world. They assert, insist, and want immediate gratification through acquisition of new experiences (Security). They develop action immediacy (Spontaneity) and may spread themselves thin (hyperactivity). They under value emotions (≠FEEL) and under develop intimacy in relationships.

Main theme Type 7	
Fear	I feel deprived and I am missing out
Need	I need to take care of my own needs
Focus	I am experience oriented and pre-occupied with activities
Strength	I learn to be Spontaneous and enthusiastic
Weakness	Hyper-activity spreads me thin while not enjoying any of it
Blindness	I jump from task to task and don't see my limitations
Vice	Gluttony, or over-doing things
Growth	Shed the idea you are missing out and enjoy the moment
Own friend	Learn to reflect and appreciate what you have
Paul Allen, Howard Stern, Billy Cristal, Elton John, Freddy Mercury, Liberace	

Healthy Sevens reduce activity involvement, learn to appreciate what they have, and become profound and insightful (5). An unhealthy Seven becomes critical and judgmental (1).

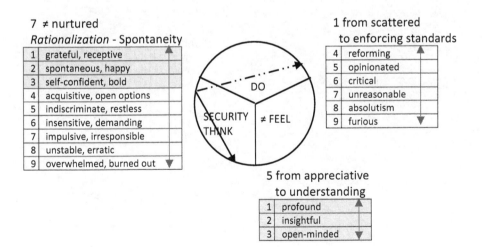

7 ≠ nurtured
Rationalization - Spontaneity

1	grateful, receptive
2	spontaneous, happy
3	self-confident, bold
4	acquisitive, open options
5	indiscriminate, restless
6	insensitive, demanding
7	impulsive, irresponsible
8	unstable, erratic
9	overwhelmed, burned out

1 from scattered
to enforcing standards

4	reforming
5	opinionated
6	critical
7	unreasonable
8	absolutism
9	furious

5 from appreciative
to understanding

1	profound
2	insightful
3	open-minded

Eight: "Who will harm me?"

Eights seek self-reliance by taking charge (Autonomy). They assert, insist, want immediate gratification. They develop a forthcoming (Candor) and confrontational attitude. They under value emotions (≠FEEL) and under develop intimacy in relationships.

Main theme Type 8	
Fear	My weaknesses will be exploited and they will harm me
Need	I need be strong and get them before they get me
Focus	I must be in charge to protect myself
Strength	I learn to say what I mean and means what I say or Candor
Weakness	Being too forthcoming leads to bluntness
Blindness	I don't consider the emotional impact I have on others
Vice	Lust, for power that is
Growth	Shed the idea you have to be in charge and cannot trust others
Own friend	Learn to trust others and be compassionate for their cause
Napoleon Bonaparte, Evel Knievel, Nancy Grace, Chris Christie, Gloria Allred	

Healthy Eights reduce their need to be in charge and develop compassion for others (2). Unhealthy Eights become dictatorial after which they withdraw out of fear for retaliation (5).

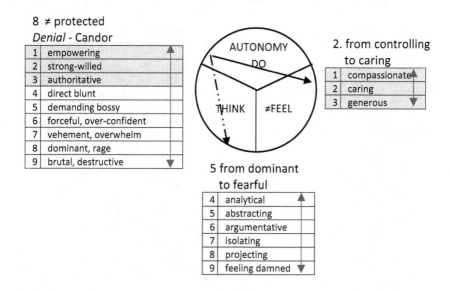

8 ≠ protected
Denial - Candor

1	empowering
2	strong-willed
3	authoritative
4	direct blunt
5	demanding bossy
6	forceful, over-confident
7	vehement, overwhelm
8	dominant, rage
9	brutal, destructive

2. from controlling to caring

1	compassionate
2	caring
3	generous

5 from dominant to fearful

4	analytical
5	abstracting
6	argumentative
7	isolating
8	projecting
9	feeling damned

Six: "What should I do?"

Sixes seek to make sense of the world and conform to prevailing morals and values of society (Security). They mediate between ideals and their conscience. They are moralizers and conform or rebel against authority. They worry about what might go wrong and learn to adhere to existing principles (Loyalty). They want others to embrace their convictions. They under value veracity and under develop judgment (≠THINK).

Main theme Type 6	
Fear	I am without support and don't know what to do
Need	I need support and guidance
Focus	I either comply or defy provided support
Strength	I develop Loyalty to my convictions
Weakness	Excess loyalty leads to blind obedience
Blindness	I may not consider veracity
Vice	Fear for loss of support
Growth	Shed the idea you need outside guidance
Own friend	Trust your own opinions and be self-guiding
Robert Blake, David Letterman, Rush Limbaugh, George W. Bush	

Healthy Sixes replace anxiety over self-doubt with peaceful optimism (9). Unhealhty Sixes become divisive and vindictive(3).

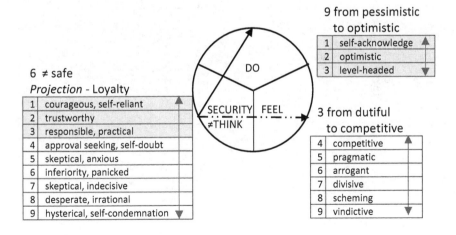

9 from pessimistic
to optimistic

1	self-acknowledge
2	optimistic
3	level-headed

6 ≠ safe
Projection - Loyalty

1	courageous, self-reliant
2	trustworthy
3	responsible, practical
4	approval seeking, self-doubt
5	skeptical, anxious
6	inferiority, panicked
7	skeptical, indecisive
8	desperate, irrational
9	hysterical, self-condemnation

DO

SECURITY FEEL
≠THINK

3 from dutiful
to competitive

4	competitive
5	pragmatic
6	arrogant
7	divisive
8	scheming
9	vindictive

One: "Is this the best solution?"

Ones seek self-reliance by setting standards for self and others (Autonomy). They mediate between ideals and their conscience. They are moralizers and adhere to personal principles (Idealism). They want others to embrace their convictions. They under value veracity and under develop judgment (≠THINK).

Main theme Type 1	
Fear	I am not good enough
Need	I must be better, even perfect
Focus	I provide personal standards
Strength	I am Idealistic
Weakness	Enforcing personal standards with emphatic certainty
Blindness	Does not acknowledge gray areas
Vice	Wrath; others not trying as hard as they do
Growth	Shed the idea others need your guidance
Own friend	Be flexible, accept opinions, enjoy life
Dr. Jack Kevorkian, George Zimmerman, H. Ross Perot, Colin Powell	

Healthy Ones are prudent, objective, and enjoy life (7). Unhealthy Ones are rigid, withdrawn, and self-tormenting (4).

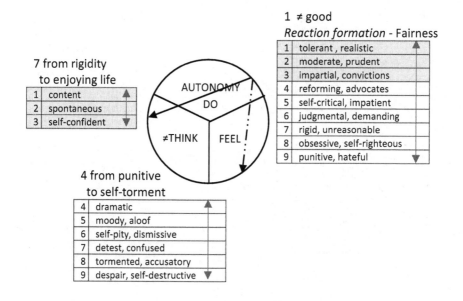

1 ≠ good
Reaction formation - Fairness

1	tolerant , realistic
2	moderate, prudent
3	impartial, convictions
4	reforming, advocates
5	self-critical, impatient
6	judgmental, demanding
7	rigid, unreasonable
8	obsessive, self-righteous
9	punitive, hateful

7 from rigidity
to enjoying life

1	content
2	spontaneous
3	self-confident

AUTONOMY
DO
≠THINK   FEEL

4 from punitive
to self-torment

4	dramatic
5	moody, aloof
6	self-pity, dismissive
7	detest, confused
8	tormented, accusatory
9	despair, self-destructive

Two: "Am I loved?"

Twos seek personal value by meeting the needs of others (Attention). They mediate between ideals and their conscience. They are moralizers and adhere to the personal principle of being good (Empathy) and want others to embrace their convictions. They under value veracity and under develop judgment (≠THINK).

Main theme Type 2	
Fear	I am not loved
Need	I need unconditional love
Focus	I must earn love and appreciation
Strength	I develop Empathy
Weakness	I provide unwanted assistance to feel needed
Blindness	I forget personal needs favoring the needs of others
Vice	Pride, in being needed
Growth	Shed the idea others need you
Own friend	Attend to your own needs before you meet the needs of others
Princess Diana, Monica Lewinsky, Richard Simmons, Patsy Ramsey, Yoko Ono	

A healthy Two provides assistance without expecting a return. They are gentle and inspiring (4). An unhealhty Two, frustrated over the lack of return for their long term efforts, becomes overinvolved, overwhelming, and even destructive (8).

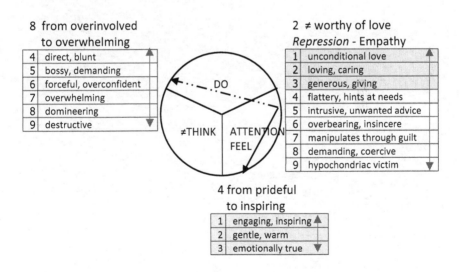

8 from overinvolved
  to overwhelming

4	direct, blunt
5	bossy, demanding
6	forceful, overconfident
7	overwhelming
8	domineering
9	destructive

2 ≠ worthy of love
Repression - Empathy

1	unconditional love
2	loving, caring
3	generous, giving
4	flattery, hints at needs
5	intrusive, unwanted advice
6	overbearing, insincere
7	manipulates through guilt
8	demanding, coercive
9	hypochondriac victim

4 from prideful
  to inspiring

1	engaging, inspiring
2	gentle, warm
3	emotionally true

Nine: "Can I tolerate this?"

Nines seek self-reliance by maintaining tranquility (Autonomy). They mediate between ideals and reality and avoid conflict (Tolerance). They withdraw to think (≠DO), weigh principles versus outcomes, and provide measured responses. They under value self and under develop their position in the world or how they fit in.

Main theme Type 9	
Fear	I fear loss of connection with others
Need	I need personal space
Focus	I must find tranquility
Strength	I learn to be Tolerant
Weakness	Excess tolerance leads to complacency
Blindness	I don't express my personal preferences
Vice	Sloth, or passive-aggressively resisting others
Growth	Shed the idea your opinions do not matter
Own friend	Learn to embrace and express what you think and want
Abraham Lincoln, Barack Obama, Ronald Reagan, Sandra Bullock	

A healthy Nine learns to express personal opinions (3) while an unhealthy Nine becomes an over-reacting hysteric (6).

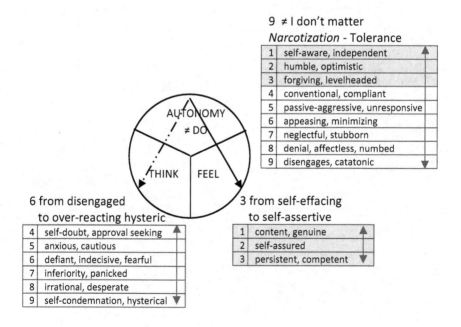

9 ≠ I don't matter
Narcotization - Tolerance

1	self-aware, independent
2	humble, optimistic
3	forgiving, levelheaded
4	conventional, compliant
5	passive-aggressive, unresponsive
6	appeasing, minimizing
7	neglectful, stubborn
8	denial, affectless, numbed
9	disengages, catatonic

AUTONOMY ≠ DO
THINK FEEL

6 from disengaged
to over-reacting hysteric

4	self-doubt, approval seeking
5	anxious, cautious
6	defiant, indecisive, fearful
7	inferiority, panicked
8	irrational, desperate
9	self-condemnation, hysterical

3 from self-effacing
to self-assertive

1	content, genuine
2	self-assured
3	persistent, competent

Four: "Am I the only one feeling this way?"

Fours seek personal value by finding their identity (Attention). They mediate between ideals and reality. They feel excluded and become different to be acknowledged (Originality). They withdraw to think (≠DO) pondering about why they are excluded. They under value self and under develop their position in the world or how they fit in.

Main theme Type 4	
Fear	I am without an identity, I feel flawed, and excluded
Need	I need to have my own identity and be included
Focus	I must distinguish myself
Strength	I learn to be Original
Weakness	I desire what others have and become chronically disappointed
Blindness	I don't acknowledge personal qualities
Vice	Envy, or coveting what others have
Growth	Shed the idea others have better qualities
Own friend	Embrace your qualities and inspire others
Melissa Etheridge, Bob Dylan, Paul Simon, Amy Winehouse	

The healthy Four develops objectivity about personal strengths and use those strengths to inspire others(1). An unhealthy Four makes others walk on egg shells (2).

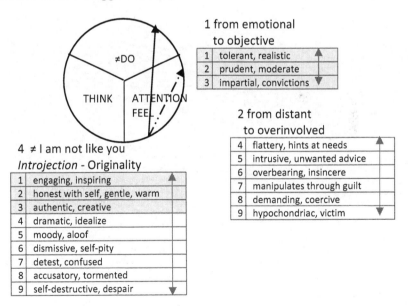

1 from emotional
to objective

1	tolerant, realistic
2	prudent, moderate
3	impartial, convictions

2 from distant
to overinvolved

4	flattery, hints at needs
5	intrusive, unwanted advice
6	overbearing, insincere
7	manipulates through guilt
8	demanding, coercive
9	hypochondriac, victim

4 ≠ I am not like you
Introjection - Originality

1	engaging, inspiring
2	honest with self, gentle, warm
3	authentic, creative
4	dramatic, idealize
5	moody, aloof
6	dismissive, self-pity
7	detest, confused
8	accusatory, tormented
9	self-destructive, despair

Five: "Is it true or not true?"

Fives seek to make sense of the world through abstract understanding (Security). They mediate between ideals and reality. They feel unacknowledged and compensate by providing specialized knowledge (Discernment). They withdraw to think (≠DO) to find understanding and their truth. They under value self and under develop their position in the world or how they fit in.

Main theme Type 5	
Fear	I am not acknowledged and my needs are not important to you
Need	I need to fit in
Focus	I must understand and provide specialized knowledge
Strength	I learn to distinguish true versus not true (Discernment)
Weakness	Over focus on learning leads to useless over-specialization
Blindness	Overthinking leads to not paying attention to what is already there
Vice	Avarice (Greed), best explained as retention of knowledge
Growth	Shed the idea you don't fit in
Own friend	Learn to participate in the world
Bobby Fisher, Bill Gates, Albert Einstein, Stephen Hawking, Neil Degrasse Tyson	

A healthy Five leads with confidence (8) whereas an unhealthy Five becomes scattered and burned out (7).

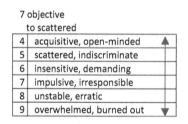

7 objective
to scattered

4	acquisitive, open-minded
5	scattered, indiscriminate
6	insensitive, demanding
7	impulsive, irresponsible
8	unstable, erratic
9	overwhelmed, burned out

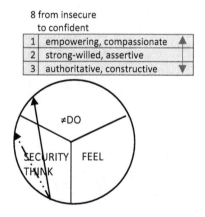

8 from insecure
to confident

1	empowering, compassionate
2	strong-willed, assertive
3	authoritative, constructive

5 ≠ acknowledged
Isolation - Discernment

1	comprehending, profound
2	insightful, fascinated
3	skillful, open-minded, uncompromising
4	knowledgeable, analytical
5	abstracting, intense, speculates
6	argumentative, intellectual arrogance
7	isolation, unstable, dark thoughts
8	insomniac, projecting, sinister
9	deranged, suicidal, feeling damned

Answers

1. One Reason means there is only one reason why we like somebody. This reason is "they make us feel good."
2. We need to Look and Listen to observe behavioral styles and listen to what they say. Identifying a distinct pattern leads to understanding a core perspective and a core need.
3. We talk most about that what is important to us.
4. Personality is a repetitive response to our internal dialogue.
5. Our perspective creates a thought, which we will express. We will act out and repeat what we know best. It becomes our destiny.
6. Born with natural abilities and influenced by our environment. We identify with our role models, develop a core perspective, a processing style, and ego defense mechanisms. We develop a behavioral and social style leading to a distinct and consistent behavioral pattern.
7. The Enneagram maps behavioral clusters and links behaviors to perspective.
8. Behavioral patterns stack like building blocks on top of each other.
9. Although the groups 378, 612, and 945 have similarities in behaviors, the Types have complete different perspectives.
10. A Wing is the Type next to your own with the most influence on your own Type. It flavors your type.
11. Autonomy or to be self-reliant; Attention or to be appreciated for who we are; Security or to feel safe with the ones we are with.
12. We assert (Fight), conform (Fear), and withdraw (Flight)
13. We are logical and methodical; emphatic and demonstrative; Positive minded and people oriented.
14. We recognize Types through perspective (Listen!) and behavioral clusters (Look!).
15. The three processing centers are head, heart, and gut. For simplicity reasons referred to as Think, Feel, and Do.

16. We process information differently. This is almost like speaking a different language leading to misinterpretation of what was said.
17. We can identify core perspectives by listening to what people say. We can recognize behavioral clusters and determine someone's Type. We can then influence with integrity and play into their strengths. We can emphasize what they need, like, want to hear, and gain another friend. We need friends to feel validated and become successful.
18. The Assertives get what they want. They assert, insist, and are prone to overstep boundaries without realizing the emotional impact they have on others. Their strengths are perseverance, spontaneity, and candor.
19. The core perspective of a Three is "I must be seen as a Success." They link self-esteem to performance acknowledgement.
20. The core perspective of a Seven is "I must stay busy to avoid anxiety." They are experience oriented and link self-esteem to acquisition of experiences and material things.
21. The core perspective of an Eight is "I must protect myself." They are self-protective by presenting themselves as strong and domineering.
22. The Dedicated and Reliable are dedicated to rules and reliable to follow through. They feel best when they conform to rules they know best. They weigh morals and values and are prone to irrational emotional reactivity. Their strengths are loyalty, idealism, and compassion.
23. The core perspective of a Six is "I don't know what to do and I don't know who to turn to." They can be authority compliant or defiant and chronically ambivalent.
24. The core perspective of a One is "I must improve the world." They set their own rules, correct self, and others. They can enforce personal standards with emphatic certainty.
25. The core perspective of a Two is "I must be good to you" to earn love and appreciation. They are well intentioned and may

provide unwanted assistance. They may become hypochondriacs to get the attention they seek.

26. The Withdrawns and Imaginatives withdraw to think and use their imagination to find solutions. They tend to overthink and are prone to procrastination. Their strengths are tolerance, self-awareness, and abstract understanding.
27. The core perspective of a Nine is "I must have tranquility." They avoid conflict and keep to themselves. They like to be alone and prefer to nap when stressed. They may become disengaged and complacent.
28. The core perspective of a Four is "I am different and therefore excluded." They must find what is missing and are prone to chronic disappointment. They may become emotionally unavailable.
29. The core perspective of a Five is "I must observe to understand the world." They need abstract understanding, are inquisitive, and information junkies. They may become unavailable by isolating themselves to find what they need to know.
30. from One to Nine: idealism, empathy, perseverance, originality, discernment, loyalty, spontaneity, candor, tolerance.
31. A weakness is "excess strength."
32. From One to Nine: emphatic certainty, provides unwanted assistance, exploitation, gets emotionally stuck, useless over-specialization, blind obedience, reckless hyper-activity, bluntness, complacency.
33. Ego-defense mechanisms are coping strategies used when confronted with conflict, stress, and discomfort.
34. We give others what we need the most because we believe others have similar needs.

References

Elfers, Marcel D.: *"We are the same; it's the details that differ."* (2015)
Hurley, Kathleen, and Dobson, Theodore: *"My best self: using the enneagram to free the soul."* (1993)
Riso, Don Richard, and Hudson, Russ: *Personality Types: Using the Enneagram for Self-Discovery* (1996)
Riso, Don Richard, and Hudson, Russ: *The wisdom of the Enneagram, the complete guide to psychological and spiritual growth for the nine personality types* (1999)
Schafer, Jack, PhD, with Karlins, Marvin, PhD: *"The Like Switch."* (2015)
Sue, David; Sue, Derald Wing, and Sue, Stanley: *Understanding abnormal behavior* 8th Edition (2006)

Made in the USA
Charleston, SC
11 July 2016